LEGAL REFORM AND BUSINESS CONTRACTS IN DEVELOPING ECONOMIES

This book advances our understanding of the role of law in the rule of law affecting commercial transactions. Julie Paquin's work on the complex relationships and influences underlying contractual performance bridges the gap between theory and practice. Although situated in the day-to-day reality of Dakar, her research illuminates the broader fabric of constraints to successful reform efforts, with findings that will help to shape future research and programming.

Wade Channell, Senior Legal Reform Advisor, USAID

Cultural Diversity and Law

Series Editor:
Prakash Shah, School of Law, Queen Mary, University of London, UK

Around the world, most states are faced with difficult issues arising out of cultural diversity in their territories. Within the legal field, such issues span across matters of private law through to public and constitutional law. At international level too there is now considerable jurisprudence regarding ethnic, religious and cultural diversity. In addition, there are several layers of legal control – from communal and religious regulation to state and international regulation. This multiplicity of norm setting has been variously termed legal pluralism, inter-legality or inter-normativity and provides a fascinating lens for academic analysis that links up to cultural diversity in new and interesting ways. The umbrella of cultural diversity encompasses various population groups throughout the world ranging from national, ethnic, religious or indigenous groupings. This series particularly welcomes work that is of comparative interest, concerning various state jurisdictions as well as different population groups.

Also in the series

Socio-Legal Integration
Polish Post-2004 EU Enlargement Migrants in the United Kingdom
Agnieszka Kubal
ISBN 978-1-4094-3700-0

Law, Religious Freedoms and Education in Europe
Edited by Myriam Hunter-Henin
ISBN 978-1-4094-2730-8

Islamic Law in Europe?
Legal Pluralism and its Limits in European Family Laws
Andrea Büchler
ISBN 978-1-4094-2849-7

The Challenges of Justice in Diverse Societies
Constitutionalism and Pluralism
Meena K. Bhamra
ISBN 978-1-4094-1928-0

Legal Reform and Business Contracts in Developing Economies

Trust, Culture, and Law in Dakar

JULIE PAQUIN
University of Ottawa, Canada

LONDON AND NEW YORK

First published 2012 by Ashgate Publishing

2 Park Square, Milton Park, Abingdon, Oxfordshire OX14 4RN
52 Vanderbilt Avenue, New York, NY 10017

Routledge is an imprint of the Taylor & Francis Group, an informa business

First issued in paperback 2020

British Library Cataloguing in Publication Data
Paquin, Julie.
Legal reform and business contracts in developing economies
: trust, culture, and law in Dakar. -- (Cultural diversity and law)
  1. Commercial law--Africa. 2. Law--Africa--International
unification. 3. Business enterprises--Law and
legislation--Senegal--Dakar. 4. Organisation pour
l'harmonisation en Afrique du droit des affaires.
  I. Title II. Series
  346.6'07-dc23

Library of Congress Cataloging-in-Publication Data
Paquin, Julie.
Legal reform and business contracts in developing economies : trust, culture, and law in Dakar
/ by Julie Paquin.
    p. cm. -- (Cultural diversity and law)
  Includes bibliographical references and index.
  ISBN 978-1-4094-4488-6 (hardback) 1. Business law--Senegal--Dakar. 2. Law reform--Senegal
--Dakar. 3. Contracts--Senegal--Dakar. 4. Law reform--Developing countries. 5. Business law--
Developing countries. I. Title.
  KTG920.P37 2012
  346.66307--dc23

                                                                                    2012026013

ISBN 978-1-4094-4488-6 (hbk)
ISBN 978-0-367-60177-5 (pbk)

To Marceline, Carl, Hugues, and Richard

Contents

Introduction

Since the end of the 1980s, the mainstream discourse about development has taken a radical turn. After a decade characterized by the failure of structural adjustment programs and neo-liberal prescriptions to generate growth in the developing world, concepts like "poverty reduction", "good governance", and "rights-based development" emerged as new buzzwords. One of the most striking phenomena in the development field has been the resurgence of interest in law. After more than 20 years spent in disrepute, legal reform has now returned to the foreground in development programs built around the concept of the rule of law. Inspired by insights from New Institutional Economics, development experts now hold that law (or "legal institutions") is a prerequisite to development. Conversely, the numerous "problems" of developing countries, including their presumed lack of commitment to democracy and their failure to "catch up" with their developed counterparts, are blamed on their legal institutions.

In both the policy and academic communities, global reform through law has now become an orthodoxy, in which the new mantra is that the "rule of law" is an essential pre-condition for development. In the last 15 years, a growing number of national and international organizations, including USAID and the World Bank, have adopted comprehensive legal reform programs. Western nations, private donors, and international aid agencies have spent billions of dollars on rule of law reforms focusing mostly on the drafting of better laws, the creation of efficient judicial institutions, and the increase of government's compliance with the law. Even though evaluations of the legal reform programs implemented so far have often not been very optimistic, they continue to be seen as a fundamental component of reform agendas aiming at establishing democratic regimes, protecting human rights, promoting economic development and fighting poverty.

As noted by Davis and Trebilcock (2008), a great deal of the debate now surrounding the use of law in development does not concern the usefulness of law reform, but how it is to be pursued. Among the criticisms leveled against current reform programs, a prominent one concerns the heavy reliance of policymakers on Western legal models rather than homegrown laws as a basis for reform. Following a well-established line of comparative law scholars, numerous commentators have underlined the close relationship between law and the social context in which it emerges and expressed doubts about the capacity of laws designed in a given environment to produce similar, or even desirable, results when transferred to a new setting.

A closer look at the current law and development agenda reveals that it fails to give full and adequate consideration to the question of the effectiveness of legal transfers. Although policymakers take care to warn against the bulk export of foreign laws and underline the need to take local conditions into account in reform design, these broad statements seem to have a limited impact on reform agendas. In the case of business law, more particularly, the reforms implemented consist essentially in the import of the "best practices" in use in the West, with a minimal degree of adaptation to local circumstances.

The present work emerged from my desire to understand the reasons underlying this failure to pay adequate consideration to the issue of the "fit" in business law reform. Pragmatic considerations undoubtedly account for part of the apparent lack of interest in the need for legal tailoring. The current context of market globalization and the focus put on foreign investment as a leading force in economic development provide powerful incentives for legal harmonization. By contributing to the creation of larger markets, regional or international integration is said to relieve producers from the need to adapt their products to different regulatory frameworks and attract the foreign investors needed for development to take place. The adoption of legal models that have the favor of those investors is thought to make the new markets more attractive to those investors, while constituting an economical alternative to their creation from scratch or their "customization", which both necessitate skills that are in short supply in developing countries.

And yet, contemporary globalization narratives hardly tell the whole story, with development programs based on the export of laws dating at least as far back as the eighteenth century. Current programs, which have become known as forming the "second law and development movement", would be better described as but the last in a series of initiatives based on a persistent and profound belief in the power of law to modify the human economic behaviors that are thought to impede economic development. From this perspective, the most surprising thing about the Second Law and Development is not the re-emergence of law as a development tool, even in light of the inefficiency of previous attempts, but the failure of its proponents to address the important charges of ethnocentrism leveled against its most immediate predecessor.

This book argues that this failure to fully consider the issue of the cultural "fit" between imported laws and receiving societies originates from a specific conceptualization of business decisions as rational, driven by self-interest, and unhindered by cultural considerations. Following this approach, business law, deemed to apply in a "market" elevated to the status of a universal ideal, is thought to be independent from other forms of law as well as the society in which business relationships take place. In the case of current business law reform programs, the overt reliance of policymakers on models of human behavior based on New

Institutional Economics has made it even easier to sweep aside potential objections based on cultural grounds. Conversely, advocates for local cultures seem to have difficulties framing arguments in favor of local cultures that do not put into question the possibility or desirability of market-based economic development. In consequence, debates around rule of law reforms are often framed in ideological rather than practical terms, and revolve around the issue of whether human rights, the rule of law or markets constitute universal ideals attainable by peoples of all culture or Western impositions of a neo-colonial character (Fitzpatrick 1993, 27; Merry 2004, 569; Mohan and Holland 2001).

Through its focus on self-interest as the essential determinant of economic behavior, the new law and development agenda implies that "cultural arguments will peel away as the hard evidence of the effects of good political institutions and property law sink in" (de Soto 2000, 225). By assuming that the spirit of capitalism is alive and well within every entrepreneur and needs only the right institutional conditions to express itself, the current agenda ignores the possibility that certain groups of people may be unable – or unwilling – to embrace "pro-development" values, and thus fails to confront the extent to which cultural change may be a prerequisite to economic development. Indeed, the notion that culture could be an impediment to legal change, or that law should aim at modifying certain undesirable cultural traits, seems to have been quasi-taboo in the law and development community for the last 30 years. The overall impression is that the new movement tries to avoid facing accusations of imperialism and ethnocentrism that were leveled against the first law and development movement, whose primary goal consisted in the transformation of legal culture and institutions through legal transfers and education (Trubek 2006, 76), by deliberately eschewing the thorny question of the level of "cultural fit" needed for transferred legal models to work in different cultural environments. The backdrop of this rhetoric is a general failure to produce a satisfactory answer to the questions of the need for cultural change and the possibility to effect it through legal education programs. Even though many of the recent publications about the role of law in development underline the need not to repeat the mistakes of the past, little attention is brought to the most important sources of these mistakes: the failure to fully consider the nature of the relationship between law and society in general, and the role played by law in business relationships in particular.

This book aims at investigating these issues by examining the potential and actual impact of imported business law on the actors operating in societies receiving those imports. Despite the current consensus that legal reform constitutes an efficient and essential tool for economic development, the empirical arguments used in support of this proposition essentially consist in the comparison of complicated and controversial country-level data. As noted by Karlan and Appel with respect to the fight against poverty, much of the work on law and development "is in a sense like bloodletting. There is a wealth of conviction and some agreement about the driving principles ... but that's about the extent of it" (Karlan and Appel 2011, 29). The statistical data and indicators currently in use also provide little information on the many factors impacting on the efficiency of the implemented reforms, including the potential role of local cultures. A better assessment of the actual impact of law reform programs requires another, more inductive, kind of approach, making room for the identification of diverse factors as well as the examination of how they interact with each other in specific situations.

Sub-Saharan Africa provides an ideal setting for these purposes. At the end of the twentieth century, the prospects for the region were bleak enough for *The Economist* to run a cover story labeling the continent as "hopeless" (*The Economist* 2000). This may change in coming years, as Africa has become the primary target of many development efforts. Upon his appointment as the new president of the World Bank in June 2005, Paul Wolfowitz even vowed to make the "world's foremost development challenge" a top priority of the Bank (World Bank 2005b). In a recent cover story, *The Economist* noted that a profound change has taken hold in Africa in the last 10 years, even while noting that the situation is "still exceedingly bleak in much of the continent" (*The Economist* 2011, 15). As of now, though, sub-Saharan Africa, which has represented a puzzle for development experts ever since the birth of the notion of development, has yet failed to garner high levels of interest among researchers, especially compared to Asia and Latin America. With little being known about the realities of businesses operating in sub-Saharan Africa, many of the assumptions underlying development programs have remained practically untested in the African context. In addition, although it is commonplace for observers to point to the existence of some inherited character flaw preventing Africans from embracing pro-development values, and to characterize the African attitude toward State law as a form of "cultural resistance" to foreign norms, the actual impact that such cultural factors might have on reform efforts curiously remains little investigated.

With respect to the study of legal reform programs, West Africa emerges as an area of particular interest within the African sub-continent. In the course of the last 20 years, a large proportion of the countries of the West African region have been engaged in an ambitious program of law reform known under the acronym OHADA.[1] Focusing on all those aspects of legislation that impact on business activity, the OHADA reform entails the application, in all the Member States of the Organization, of a series of uniform acts that purport to create a "modern"

---

1   OHADA stands for "Organisation pour l'harmonisation en Afrique du droit des affaires." The English equivalent, OHBLA (Organisation for the Harmonisation of Business Law in Africa) is seldom used.

legal framework that would attract investments. Overtly based on French law, the reform was primarily designed to serve the needs of foreign, and primarily French, firms interested in doing business in the region, and makes little, if any, room for the kind of culture-conscious adjustments that could prevent further resistance to the reform at the local level.

Little is known on the actual impact of the OHADA reform on local business activity. The book contributes to bridging this gap by examining whether, and how, OHADA has had an impact on local businesses operating in one specific setting within the region covered by the reform, i.e. the city of Dakar, in Senegal.

Senegal, which is an important member of the OHADA initiative, figured on the World Bank's list of the world's top ten reformers for 2007–2008 (World Bank 2008, 1). The country nevertheless still ranked among the worst performers of 2012 in terms of the "ease of doing business", coming 154th out of the 183 economies surveyed by the Bank (World Bank 2012a, 6). Departing from the current focus on cross-national indicators of performance, this book examines the impact of the reforms implemented in Senegal through the eyes of the people most directly concerned with them. It constitutes a humble attempt to give a voice to seldom-heard African entrepreneurs about the development of their country and the potential role of law in this process. By departing from "expert views" of the West African economic and legal situation, the book sheds a new light on the relationship between formal law and the day-to-day operations of small- and medium-sized firms operating in developing economies. As such, it provides insights of relevance not only to Senegal and West Africa, but also to all developing countries seeking to align their laws with the "best practices" identified by aid institutions.

Although this book tackles a classic comparative law issue – the transferability of law – its approach differs profoundly from those traditionally taken by legal scholars. First, the emphasis is not put on the normative content of legal transfers and their compatibility with existing legal institutions, but on their actual impact or lack of impact on end-users. Secondly, the impact of the legal norms is not analyzed in terms of the efficiency of the implementation mechanisms put in place, including by measuring levels of knowledge of a law, the "barriers" to its effective application, or the quality of judicial decisions. Rather, this study resorts to a bottom-up approach in which phenomena acquire or fail to acquire a legal character according to how they are perceived by those involved in them. The focus is put on the relationships between the diverse formal and informal modes of ordering at the disposal of legal actors, and the logics behind their choice to apply one set of norms over another in specific situations. The pluralist approach to normativity taken in this work precludes any *a priori* distinction between "law" and "non law", and considers State law as being on an equal footing with other modes of social ordering. The emphasis is then put on the interaction between these modes and the conditions under which certain ones come to take precedence over others.

The study conducted in Dakar focused on the contracting practices and dispute resolution preferences of small- and medium-sized enterprises (SMEs) operating in Dakar, whose situation remains largely undocumented. It shows that neither the inefficiency of local legal institutions nor cultural "barriers" to litigation are the primary factor accounting for the little use that Dakar SMEs make of law in the resolution of their business disputes. The impact of cultural factors on attitudes toward imported law, although non negligible, emerges as much more nuanced than cultural theories would suggest. In addition, accounts of how contractual disputes emerge and are solved in Dakar and the various factors accounting for the decisions made by economic actors operating in the area raise important doubts about the central role generally ascribed to law in contracting behavior. The book thus calls for a reconsideration of current law and development theory and, more generally, the role of contract law in business decisions.

In Chapter 1, a short review of the practice of law and development in sub-Saharan Africa is presented, with a view to examining how the diverse waves of economic development programs implemented in the region solved or eschewed the thorny issue of the fit between local conditions and the legal models imported from more developed economies. Chapter 2 takes a closer look at the notion of contract enforcement and the role it plays in the current law and development agenda. Chapters 3 and 4 present the business climate prevailing in Dakar and the data gathered among small- and medium-sized enterprises operating in the area. Chapter 5 discusses the implications of the data gathered for current theories about the nature and role of informal contract enforcement mechanisms and business networks and the importance of cultural factors in legal reform, and presents some policy and research implications arising out of the research described in this book.

Chapter 1
Law, Development and Culture in Africa

The emergence of "law and development" is inseparable from the birth of the notion of "development" as a field of knowledge and practice. Although "development theory", in its modern sense, is routinely thought to have emerged in Western thought in the aftermath of World War II, following the reconstruction of Europe under the Marshall Plan, the notion that "progress" can be brought from outside to less advanced peoples dates as far back as the nineteenth century, a period when "those who saw themselves as developed, believed that they could act to determine the process of development for others deemed less-developed" (Cowen and Shenton 1995, 28). During the colonial period, it was widely believed that colonized peoples could, and would, more or less gradually "develop" under the guidance of their benevolent conquerors. Although the term "development" itself shared the ground with others such as "civilization", "evolution", or "progress", it was far from unknown. Many of the practices that will later come to be associated with "development theory" were also in use in colonial times, including the provision of international assistance in the form of capital and expertise.

As the short historical review of law and development in West Africa that follows will show, decolonization did not entail the creation of development theory as much as its adaptation to a changing political context. Even as modernization replaced civilization as the official objective of development initiatives, the expected end results of both processes remained essentially the same, i.e. the transformation of non-Western societies – and their laws – along Western lines. Similarly, the subsequent failure of modernization efforts to drive development in the former European colonies entailed a reconsideration of the means previously used for this purpose, but little discussion of the endpoint of the development process. Moreover, at no time did policymakers contemplate serious difficulties convincing Africans to resort to "modern" laws to regulate their business activities and contracts.

Civilizing Africa: Customary Law under Association and Indirect Rule

For many historians, what came to be known as the "scramble for Africa" signals the formal beginning of a new age of empire, in which law and order were to be one of the most precious markers of civilization brought by European powers to their new "subjects". But the law imposed by colonial rulers did not reproduce its metropolitan model. Although there was some measure of legal transfers from Europe to Africa, essentially in issues involving Europeans, colonial law developed into a quite distinct system.

The elaboration of colonial legal systems was made in a piecemeal and haphazard fashion, leading to the adoption of a hybrid law incorporating concepts of European and African origins. It has been commonplace for at least 80 years to describe the French and British approaches in colonial Africa as representing opposite trends in colonial policy, with debates on the respective merits and real nature of French and British policies dating as far back as the colonial endeavor itself. And yet, the classical opposition between French and British colonial policies tends to overestimate the differences and underestimate the commonalities between colonial policies. This is not meant to deny that there were disagreements on the nature and objectives of the colonial mission. But rather than between French and British styles of administration, the ideological debate that took place on colonial policy issues would be better described as one between early "assimilationist" ideas and later "associationist" ones.

The origins of the concept of assimilation can be traced far back in the history of European thought, to a belief, derived from the Christian tradition of proselytism, that cultural superiority carried an obligation to civilize the barbarian. According to Curtin, this belief, which he calls "conversionism", was broadly dominant in Western imperial thought during the first half of the nineteenth century and long prevailed among both French and British thinkers (Curtin 1971, xix). Conversionism was especially attractive to the French and its French version, the doctrine of Assimilation, is indeed considered by many as the traditional colonial doctrine of France.

Although one can find expressions of the assimilation spirit, principally in religious terms, under the *ancien régime*, it became an important element of French colonial policies only around the French Revolution, when it came to be translated in terms of political assimilation. In line with eighteenth-century Enlightenment philosophy and its belief in Reason and universal human equality, it defined humanity as being of a single origin; inequalities were considered superficial and resulting from education. At the legal level, the doctrine had two major implications: first, all French nationals were to be treated alike and granted full citizenship; secondly, French law was to apply to all of them. As the logical consequence of universalist thinking, the French laws that had allowed France to attain a superior degree of civilization were to be applied without distinction in its new territories. That being said, one must be careful not to overstate the role of the doctrine of Assimilation on French policies. Expressions of doubt about the basic premise of Assimilation, i.e. the fundamental unity of the human race, and, consequently, about the adequacy of Assimilation as a tenable colonial policy, have always been present in French colonial discourse and, the doctrine also had a limited impact in practice. Under the First, Second, and Third Republics, legislation was adopted that extended the political rights of Frenchmen to a few West Africans and West Indians and provided for the political representation of colonies in the metropolitan assemblies. But those assimilating measures were seen as appropriate only for the colonies that existed in 1848, and not to those lesser-known, exotic places "habités par des populations dont les moeurs paraissent si bizarres"[1] (Deschamps 1953, 122). Assimilation was on the whole "a mere fantasy" (Davidson 1978, 98) – and even this fantasy could not be sustained for long.

In the last half of the nineteenth century, the importance of conversionism in imperial thought steadily decreased. In France, the charge against Assimilation culminated with the publication of Léopold de Saussure's *Psychologie de la colonisation française dans ses rapports avec les sociétés indigènes*, which emphasized the importance of hereditary factors in the evolution of different peoples and the resulting incapacity of people from different races to evolve along the same lines. Ten years later, French imperial theorist Jules Harmand wrote *Domination et colonisation*, in which he established the main tenets of what became the new doctrine of Association. For Harmand, conquest was justified by the moral superiority of the conquerors, who could be absolved from their crime by becoming *bons tyrans*, i.e. avoiding the use of force and working to ensure the well-being of the conquered peoples and make domination more bearable. For these purposes, colonial powers were to leave indigenous people to evolve in their own way, touching only very lightly their habits and traditions.

A similar evolution in thought from conversionist to associationist ideas took place in nineteenth-century Great Britain. As noted by Darby, it increasingly became accepted that the progress of colonized peoples would entail an extended process of change "and that it was necessary to work through the indigenous structures of authority and cultural patterns" (Darby 1987, 43). Indirect Rule, the British version of France's Association, was born. In 1922, Lord Frederick Lugard, who had been Governor General of Nigeria from 1914 to 1919, codified the rule in his book *The Dual Mandate in Tropical Africa*. Lugard defined the duty

---

1 Inhabited by people whose habits seem so strange.

of England as to bring "to the dark places of the earth, the abode of barbarism and cruelty, the torch of culture and progress, while ministering to the material needs of our own civilization" (Lugard 1965, 618). For Lugard, even the most capable of all Africans would, if left to themselves, revert to the state of misrule and tyranny in which they were found by the British. The happiness of African people therefore depended on the tutelage of Europeans. But rather than imposing a universal model of development, Lugard saw the colonizers' mission as one of "leading the backward races, by their own efforts, in their own way, to raise themselves to a higher plane of social organization" (Lugard 1965, 215). Instead of British rule, he favored "a system of native rule under the guidance and control of the British staff", whose function he saw as "primarily educative" (Lugard 1965, 228).

Of the many factors accounting for the ideological shift from Assimilation to Association and Indirect Rule, political considerations have traditionally been considered the most important. Since the implementation of European legal institutions would have required important resources that were not available for that purpose, colonial powers came to believe that the success of their enterprise necessitated the cooperation of the native populations, which itself depended on a certain degree of decentralization and the maintenance of indigenous institutions, however uncivilized they were. There also was a certain feeling of disappointment with the results of earlier assimilation measures taken in Algeria, India and the West Indies. In addition, most of the new colonies were unfavorable to European immigration and hardly lent themselves to the assimilation policies used in older colonies of settlement. In other words, legal dualism was an efficient means to ensure domination through decentralization. From this perspective, the shift from direct to indirect rule was, in Mamdani's terms, a "shift in perspective from the zeal of a civilizing mission to a calculating preoccupation with holding power" (Mamdani 1996, 286).

But the switch to associationist ideas cannot be entirely accounted for in political terms. As shown by the implementation, by colonial rulers, of numerous laws that aroused a vast amount of resistance without bringing direct benefit to them, domination was not the only goal pursued by colonial powers. More than a shift from civilization to domination, the rise of associationist ideas might signal a more profound redefinition of civilization mission, under which straightforward Europeanization was replaced by new "civilizing" methods taking into account the close relationship between law and the society in which it applies. Although Associationists still saw themselves as having a major role to play in the development of Africa and Africans, their new conceptions of progress as a continuation of a race-specific past departed from earlier visions of evolution as a straightforward process of westernization. For colonial theorist Lucy Mair, e.g. in trying to impose foreign legal schemes to conquered peoples, the colonial powers had ignored the processes of adaptation to external change in which social evolution consists: "[b]ringing with them a culture separated by centuries from that to which it is introduced, they have sought to substitute for the evolution by which they themselves reached it a series of strokes of the pen" (Mair 1936, 6). The imposition of a uniform legal framework to different races, to the extent that it proved possible at all, could only be envisioned in the very long term. The import of colonial law should thus be made incrementally and carefully, in response to the changes already made in a given society, rather than as a way to drive such changes.

The belief of colonial rulers in legal dependency suggested that they were "to govern not by force or rule of law but by using patience, diligence and knowledge, by taking into account people's will, fears and interests in order to use them and reach the objectives desired" (Dimier 2002, 172). Reforms needed to be introduced gradually, "in a direction where the need for change is really felt, and the institutions affected will gradually, almost imperceptibly, adapt themselves to it" (Mair 1936, 274). In short, the constraint of circumstances was to replace the constraint of the ruler. The "moral betterment" of Africans (i.e. their transformation into more civilized versions of themselves) was to derive essentially from the manipulation of external circumstances "so that the logic of economic necessity presents itself in new terms" (Mair 1936, 276). Similarly, for French colonial thinker Jules Harmand, colonial legislative policy must "être tout d'abord surtout économique, et se subordonner à ses effets économiques"[2] (Harmand 1910, 168). Colonial rulers should concentrate on creating the conditions necessary for commercial and industrial transactions; with such transactions giving birth in turn to new ideas and wants, economic development would occur naturally, along with the moral development following from it (de Saussure 1899, 306).

Those new understandings of the relationship between law, culture, and social change involved a change of attitude toward the local customs found in the colonies. In colonial theory, the coexistence of local and imported institutions came to be seen as a necessary step in the evolution process. The existence of dual legal regimes was seen as a temporary feature, a compromise that needed to be made in order to facilitate the transition of the colonies to a more evolved state of development. In theory, the results of the evolution process undertaken by colonized peoples could not be predicted; yet, for many, European law clearly remained the model that African law was to imitate.

---

2   Be conceived first and foremost in economic terms and depend on its economic effects.

The preservation of African law in colonial regimes was not an objective in itself as much as a means to provide a stable basis of rules upon which a more civilized, modern legal system could be built. For this purpose, the protection granted to local customs naturally excluded the protection of rules likely to endanger the success of the colonial mission. Any customary norm incompatible with the basic norms of justice and morality that were at the heart of the civilizing enterprise was held invalid. In British West Africa, even the most generous provisions concerning the applicability of African law specified that only those customs not repugnant to "natural justice, equity, and good conscience" were concerned (Allott 1960a, 158). Similarly, the decrees concerning the judicial organization of the French West African colonies usually provided that local customs applied "en tout ce qu'elles n'ont pas de contraire aux principes de la civilisation française"[3] (Solus 1927, 304). Local customs were also subordinate to the laws adopted for the colonies. In British West Africa, statutory provisions on incompatibility provided that African law applied only insofar as it was not inconsistent or incompatible with ordinances, regulations, or rules, or "the law" in force. In the French colonies, the notion of "ordre public colonial"[4] developed by legal theorist Henri Solus provided that legislation could be adopted and prevail over customary law in all cases where the colonial power considered it to be essential for the successful fulfillment of the work of colonization (Solus 1927, 303). The scope of African law was thus progressively restricted as the use of written legislation became increasingly widespread in both French and British West Africa, initially in the domains directly related to the imposition of colonial rule, such as public administration and penal law, and, later on, in fields seen as essential to the colonial endeavor, such as taxation and labor law.

The notions of "repugnancy" and "incompatibility" allowed for the exclusion of certain African norms or sets of norms on the assumption that their application would have impeded the progress of the civilization mission. But there were also more subtle ways in which African law could be excluded. In the same way as colonial powers believed that Africans should retain their own law under colonial rule, it was evident for them that Europeans could not be judged in native courts and in accordance with African standards. European laws to which they were accustomed were thus made applicable in the colonies. African law continued to apply, but only in parallel with another set of rules, making it necessary to determine which rules were applicable in any given case. In the British West African colonies, the primary criterion used for this purpose was race or descent, defined either in general terms, e.g. where legislation provided for the application

---

3   As long as they do not contradict the principles underlying French civilization.
4   Colonial public order.

of customary law to all "Africans", "natives", persons of "a race of Africa", or in a more specific manner, where certain peoples or countries were listed. A subsidiary test was the mode of life test, which was mainly used to determine whether persons "not widely separated from the Africans by race or custom" were to be treated like Africans (Allott 1970, 196). As for corporations, even those whose members were all Africans, were not subject to customary law and courts, except on the same terms as other non-Africans (Allott 1970, 192). In cases between Africans and non-Africans, English law was usually to apply, except where the matter was within the exclusive jurisdiction of the native courts, and where it appeared to the court that substantial injustice would be done to either party by a strict adherence to the rules of English law (Elias 1962, 218–20). In the French colonies, the basic distinction was between citizens and non-citizens. Except for the inhabitants of the Four Communes of Senegal, the acquisition of French citizenship by Africans was not a right but a privilege, and implied a renunciation of all the benefits deriving from one's personal status. In relations between citizens and non-citizens, the metropolitan status, being "le statut français normal et le plus élevé, le statut français de droit commun" [the normal and highest French status, the French common law status] was to prevail (Rolland and Lampué 1931, 235).

The cases in which African law was applicable were also restricted by the possibility for Africans or non-citizens to opt for colonial law, either expressly or implicitly, by merely entering into a particular kind of transaction. For example, section 19 of the *Gold Coast Supreme Court Ordinance 1876* provided that:

> No party shall be entitled to claim the benefit of any local law or custom, if it shall appear either from express contract or from the nature of the transactions out of which any suit or question may have arisen, that such party agreed that his obligations in connection with which transactions should be regulated exclusively by English law (cited in Allott 1970, 123).

The overall effect of such provisions was that, even between Africans, African law applied only "where the nature of the claim or charge (or of the transaction out of which they arise) [was] such as to connect the case with customary, rather than with any other system of law" (Allott 1960a, 193). Similarly, in French colonial law, Africans could be held to have implicitly opted for the application of French rules by entering into a transaction said to be unknown to African law (Dareste 1931, 393). More generally, as the common law of the land, colonial law was to apply on a subsidiary basis whenever African law was silent or held insufficient to deal with the matter before the court (Dareste 1931, 395), making colonial law the only one applicable to the dispute (Elias 1962, 218).

Conceived as a custom dating from immemorial time, African law was considered able to deal with the various aspects of "traditional" African life that pre-dated the colonial endeavor, but not with the new realities and relationships produced by the colonization process. Thus, for Phillips, if customary law was "in practice mainly confined to the sphere of private law – and in particular to family relations, succession, and immoveable property – the reason [was] likely to be, not that the customary law on other subjects fail[ed] to satisfy the basic condition of 'applicability', but rather that it [was] non-existent or at best in an inchoate state" (Phillips 1956, 91). The insufficiency of local customs was "la conséquence inéluctable et l'accessoire nécessaire de l'oeuvre de colonisation" [an inescapable consequence and essential part of the colonization work] (Solus 1927, 294).

One domain in which customary law was most likely to be held silent was in contractual matters, where, according to Chanock, African customs were seen "as a collection of unusable ideas that incorporated the collective responsibility for debt, lacking ways of enforcing contracts or bringing disputes to an end" (Chanock 1992, 293). Whereas it was recognized that African law could evolve, and was in fact evolving in response to the increasing individualization of traditionally collectivist societies (Robert 1955, 53), it was not the case with respect to contract matters. Despite the official preservation of local contract rules, imported French or English law was most likely to be applied by judges in contractual disputes (Decottignies 1962, 175–76, Date-Bah 1973, 257).

The recognition of African law and institutions by colonial powers was driven by their view that there were serious impediments to legal transfers between societies with very different cultural backgrounds and levels of evolution. Rather than an instrument of change, law came to be seen as a reflection of local cultures and the alignment of the laws of the colonies with those of the metropolis as resulting from a long process of social transformation. But, as the attitude of colonial theorists and administrators toward customary contract law illustrates, the principle of legal dependency had a limited impact in practice: it was only in "traditional" matters with close links to religious beliefs and values that the immemorial practices of African law were expected to evolve. In all other matters, African law was at best a mere remnant of a disappearing past with no possible relevance in a new world of opportunities. The preservation of local rules also aimed at preserving public order, by preventing the negative reactions that could arise from colonial encroachment in "sensitive" matters. It thus had little justification in matters where little resistance to imported rules could be expected. The assumed "cosmopolitan" nature of contract law (Solus 1927, 274) allowed colonial rulers to consider their own laws as a-cultural and presenting no threat to African social, political and religious orders. Whereas the close relationship between legal institutions and social life was recognized in all matters considered "traditional", legal instrumentalism still carried the day in those matters seen as bearing little relation to local cultures, such as contract law. Some cultural change was a prerequisite to the adoption of Western legal models in both "traditional" and non-traditional matters. In the latter case, though, no lengthy process of evolution was foreseen: without any local custom dealing in such matters, Africa was considered a blank slate upon which colonial rulers could imprint their own rules. It was thought that Africans would just switch from one model to another as they became emancipated from their communities, engaged with new types of activities and assimilated the progressive values of the colonizers.

Modernizing Africa: Traditional Law in Modern States

Shifts in British and French colonial policies started to be visible from the second part of the 1940s. With independence becoming increasingly unavoidable, colonial powers became less interested in the exploitation of the colonies and more concerned with managing the process of decolonization. Whereas Indirect Rule and Association aimed at mitigating the consequences of the changes taking place in the colonies, it was now thought that "native" societies had already undergone such considerable transformations that "more conscious and collective actions in preparing the indigenous peoples for industrial and political life" were needed (Lee 1967, 5). On the legal side, the period saw significant progress in the spheres of teaching, research and reform, the main emphasis being on the reform of political and judicial institutions, including the replacement of the native courts with non-traditional judicial institutions.

The African leaders who succeeded colonial rulers following independence had a more ambitious goal, i.e. the transformation of the more or less diverse groups that lived on the territory of the newly created States into single nations. Having inherited the dual legal systems established by the colonial powers, African States saw the multiplicity of laws as a divisive factor that had to be eliminated or controlled. The plural legal systems, which also symbolized the discrimination against Africans that had characterized the colonial regimes, had to disappear in favor of a single, unified system acceptable to all. The major question remained of what elements would come to compose this new unified law. The imperative of nation-building, which also involved stimulating national pride and breaking from the influence of European institutions, had implications in the legal sphere: the new law had to be distinctly African – a "law that in its benign incarnation would reflect the experiences and aspirations of African societies and the African people" (Chibundu 1997, 184).

"Law and development" in post-independence Africa thus entailed defining what it meant to be a "modern African", and what role the diverse local customs would play within a national, modern legal system. Underlining the need for law to be adapted to the social context, some argued for the preservation in the legal system of a non-codified customary law that would adapt itself to changing circumstances (Gluckman 1966; Schiller 1968). For most, however, reforms were urgently needed and immediate action required (Tunc 1966). Decisions had to be made as to which elements of customary law would be allowed to survive in the new legal systems.

These debates took place in the context of the Cold War, a period when international "development" was seen as a means to ensure international stability and the proper functioning of the international economic system as well as preventing "underdeveloped" countries from falling into communist hands. This period saw specialists from diverse fields attempting to devise appropriate theories to account for the existence of different development levels among nations. Nineteenth-century evolutionism, which had been displaced in anthropology by Malinowski's functionalism and its concomitant belief in cultural relativism, was then regaining the lost ground, and the old evolutionary/conversionist ideas of development as a universal process were soon in the forefront again under the new label of "modernization".

The return in force of evolutionism in development thought is best illustrated by the broad influence of a book by the American economist Walt Whitman Rostow called *The Stages of Economic Growth* (1960), which was to acquire cult status in the development community and form the basis for the emergence of the theory of development as "modernization. Contrary to colonial theorists, for whom all societies followed distinct paths and the endpoint of evolution could not be predicted, modernization theorists considered the differences among nations as mere quantitative gaps that could be bridged through economic growth. Under the economic lens, all societies were on a single "progressive" track leading to the creation of economic, political, social and legal institutions similar to those of the West.

Lawyers were among the last to jump on the modernization bandwagon. In the 1960s, specialists from diverse legal sub-fields joined together to form what came to be called the "law and development movement". These new legal experts had no clearly stated theory on which to rest their interventions. They were, according to Friedman, in a curious "twilight world", operating on the basis of unstated assumptions that "some legal systems are not suited to development, or stand in the way of progress, or are archaic, or outdated, or simply inadaptable" (Friedman 1969, 13–14). In line with the dominant modernization paradigm, they rested their intervention on "legal liberalism", a concept created on the basis of some of Max Weber's ideas about legal rationality. Under this theory, development was conceived of as a universal process at the end of which all societies were to present the characteristics of Western modern societies, including their legal institutions. In this process, law was to act as a causal factor of development, by putting in place the institutions necessary for change to occur. The adoption of a modern legal framework was seen as essential to development, and "[t]he Third World [...] assumed to be doomed to underdevelopment until it adopt[ed] a modern Western legal system" (Trubek 1982, 11).

From such a perspective, the balance between the African and Western elements that would form the new laws clearly tipped in favor of the Western heritage from the beginning. The possibility of accommodating some elements of "traditional" culture was admitted, but only as long as it did not compromise the modernization process. As Kéba M'Baye, who later played a major role in the adoption of the OHADA reform, remarked at the time, following initial calls for a return to the roots of African law, local customs were found unworthy of the respect paid to them (M'Baye 1966, 147). As the reflection of the very social organization that the new states intended to transform (Stoufflet 1962, 251), local customs were often thought to constitute impediments to the transformation of African society. Thus, despite declarations about the need for an authentic African law, the law of the new African states was essentially a core of Western law, with the input of customary law being generally limited to specific domains such as marriage, successions, and land law (Blanc-Jouvan 1977). Only a few adaptations considered necessary to account for the particular economic and social local conditions were made, as with the introduction of new provisions on contracts made by illiterates in the Senegalese Code of Obligations (Farnsworth 1964).

Having established the proper balance to be maintained between imported and customary norms, policymakers had to ensure the smooth transition from "customary" to "modern" law. Social change being a complex and often lengthy process, "modern" law was not expected to reach full effectiveness right from the moment of its introduction. For many, this did not constitute an impediment to immediate legal reform. Believing in the aspirational power of law, they thought that, in societies looking forward to effecting profound transformation, law had to show the way forward. For M'Baye, e.g.

> une codification peut être, soit la constatation, de ce qui est, soit l'instauration de ce qui doit être. Dans les sociétés en voie de développement, [la loi] doit attirer la révolution. [codification may state what already exists, or what has to become. In developing societies, the law must bring revolution] (M'Baye 1966, 147).

From this perspective, it was unavoidable for law to be disconnected from local social conditions (Stoufflet 1962). One proposed way to mitigate the negative consequences of the inescapable chasm between law and society was to give judges the power to use the new law as a guide to decisions rather than as binding rules, and apply it in a flexible manner, taking into account the local social realities. Despite its negative impact on legal security, it was thought that such a system could be tolerated for a time "if it would help to insure that the transplanted laws are not rejected by the receiving body before they have had an opportunity to become well-rooted" (Beckstrom 1973, 580). The gradual implementation of reform was also presented by some as the best avenue to manage the process of change: it would have the advantage of making law in advance of society, and thus able to play its instrumental role, but not so much in advance that it risked becoming a pure "fantasy law" (Schiller 1966, 200) with no bearing on reality. For example, David (1963) proposed that the Ethiopian Civil Code initially apply to a restricted set of legal operations, before being extended to other spheres. Another option was to introduce modern law as an optional regime, allowing litigants to choose between the new and the old laws during a certain period of time.

Despite some disagreement concerning the weight to be given to local customs and the transformatory power of law, the experts involved in the modernization of African legal systems basically all agreed on at least one thing: the future of African contract law. In line with Maine's (1861) idea that the progress of society involved a shift for status to contract, African law was generally considered undeveloped in the field of contracts (Nwabueze 1966, 184). For Elias, "the indigenous conceptions in this field have proved inadequate both to modern commerce and to modern industrial expansion" (Elias 1962, 142) and did not form an adequate basis for the development of a new contract law. Similarly, for Decottignies, the imperatives of economic development required first and foremost the adoption of a law of contract well adapted to the needs of developing countries:

> Croissance économique et efficacité juridique, les deux idées se complètent admirablement. Car, il ne saurait y avoir de croissance économique durable sans une législation du développement en matière de contrats et obligations. [Economic development and legal efficiency are complementary. There can be no sustainable economic development without a development-oriented law on contracts and obligations] (Decottignies 1962, 172–3).

Even those most committed to the preservation of African customary law, such as anthropologist Max Gluckman, were in favor of the immediate replacement of local customs with contract law rules fitted for a modern economy:

I think immediate instruction in the elements of a modern law of contract is most essential, since existing law is adequate to deal with other fields of relations, but not with the expanding commerce between previously unrelated persons ... it is mainly in the field of contract that traditional African law seems to lack the principles, doctrines and concepts which are appropriate to the modern world. Traditional law seems able to develop in the Law of Persons (Gluckman 1966, 73).

In addition, no one seriously contested that contract law was a cosmopolitan, technical field, which posed no threat to African traditions, and in which legal imports raised no particular challenge. The universal character of the modernization process suggested that, at least in economic matters, there was no alternative path to development. Western laws were not only required but also largely independent from any specific cultural heritage, and posed no threat to the "African modern identity" in the making. That meant, most conveniently, that the most important laws for development could be exported easily to any setting. For Schaeffer, e.g.

L'expérience tend d'ailleurs à démontrer que ce qui est indispensable au développement est généralement 'réceptible', et que ce qui n'est pas reçu n'est généralement pas nécessaire au développement. [Experience has shown that what is essential to development is generally transferable and that what is not transferable is generally not required for development] (Schaeffer 1974, 326).

The tide of legal reform of the 1960s started to slow down as the 1970s approached and disappointing results kept coming. After 1975, Third World countries tended to look more and more for external, rather than internal, factors to account for their enduring state of "underdevelopment". Third World leaders, who previously were eager to implement the recommendations of the legal missionaries, were increasingly turning to dependency theory and pressing for a new international law of development. The first law and development movement was officially declared dead in 1974, less than 15 years after its birth, when Trubek and Galanter, two of its leading figures, published an official post-mortem (Trubek and Galanter 1974). During its short and tumultuous life, its proponents had passed from an unfettered enthusiasm to a state of crisis that threatened the very existence of the new field. As funding for law and development projects dried up, most legal scholars previously involved in the field turned to domestic or international economic relations issues. By the late 1970s, the golden era of voluntary borrowing of legal models graciously provided by Western benefactors was over.

In the 1980s, neo-classical prescriptions came to replace the previously dominant Keynesian model. This period, which was later labeled "the lost decade for development" (Esteva 1992,16) was marked by the adoption of structural adjustment programs aimed at correcting the ballooning deficits of the Third World. Loans made to developing countries were conditional on their commitment to reform inappropriate public policies. In this way, the international financial institutions came to exert control over a wide range of domestic issues, including legal and judicial reform, essentially with a view to creating a favorable investment climate for foreign investors. However, the results achieved by these policy prescriptions proved disappointing in terms of growth rates and macro-economic stability, while leading to widening inequalities and political instability, combined with persistently high levels of poverty.

The realization that SAPs carried undesirable social consequences that undermined economic growth led to a reconsideration of the role played by the state in economic development. At the end of the 1980s, concerns with the role of government in development started to gain prominence in the development sphere. They culminated in 1989 with the publication of the widely influential World Bank's report titled "Sub-Saharan Africa: From Crisis to Sustainable Growth", which categorically identified the source "underlying the litany of Africa's development problems" as "a crisis of governance" (World Bank 1989, 60). Three years later, the Bank confirmed this turn by declaring good governance "an essential complement to sound economic policies" (World Bank 1992, 1). The table was set for the rebirth of "law and development".

Reforming Investment Climates: Informal Law in Efficient Markets

The Second Law and Development Movement arose from the realization by economic development agencies that markets need the right institutional conditions to be in place before they can develop. In David Trubek's words (Trubek 2006, 86), its reform agenda arose from a "curious amalgam" of the project for democracy developed by the human right movements of the 1970s and 1980s with the market-building project of development experts, under the common umbrella of the "rule of law". In the course of the 1990s and 2000s, the movement evolved somewhat, leading Trubek and Santos to distinguish the recent beginning of a "third moment" in law and development (Trubek and Santos 2006, 3). The main characteristic of the "new" law and development agenda nevertheless remains the combination of a clear recognition of the role of the state in development with a strong commitment to market liberalism and the "Washington consensus". While it is now acknowledged that "[d]evelopment – economic, social, and sustainable – without an effective State is impossible", it remains evident that "States should work to complement markets, not replace them" (World Bank 1997, 15). State interventions should contribute to the creation of an appropriate system of incentives allowing private firms to function efficiently. The job of governments is to provide an adequate institutional infrastructure in support of markets, including effective laws and the legal institutions to implement them.

The strong belief that well-functioning law and justice institutions and a government bound by the rule of law are important to economic, political and social development has caused legal reforms to return to center stage in the development agenda. Using the work of Nobel prize-winner Douglass North and other New Institutional economists as a theoretical basis, the World Bank has played a key role in the development of a set of arguments supporting the implementation of development programs based on legal reform. These arguments have now found support in a growing body of studies purporting to establish the existence of a causal relationship between legal factors and economic indicators. The Bank has again been a major actor in the generation of various statistical analyses whose results are commonly cited in academic work as well as in policy publications advocating legal reform, and which seem, at first glance, to provide compelling evidence of the causal role of law in economic development.

Taking roots in the work of Ronald Coase (1937), New Institutional Economics (NIE) developed to address the failure of the neoclassical model to account for persistent and widening disparities in wealth. NIE proponents hold that the neoclassical result of efficient markets is obtained only when it is costless to transact. Rejecting the neoclassical assumptions of perfect information and unbounded rationality, they assume that, because individuals have incomplete information and limited mental capacity, they incur transaction costs in gathering information, negotiating, monitoring, and enforcing their property rights and contracts. In consequence, while they agree with Adam Smith that economic growth stems from gains from trade and increasing specialization and division of labor, they do not see such gains as automatic. Societies benefit from trade or specialization only if the transaction costs incurred in the process of exchange are lower than the benefits they derive from that exchange. Economic growth can be achieved only by reducing these transaction costs, which are determined by the many "institutions" that reduce uncertainty by creating a stable (although not necessarily efficient) structure for human interaction.

The NIE notion of "institution" is a very broad one: it encompasses all human-devised forms of constraints that shape human interaction, including formal rules as well as informal elements such as social norms and codes of behavior. According to North, successful economies are characterized by the evolution of their institutions, which has allowed them to move from simple to more complex forms of contracting. At first, the general pattern of exchange consisted in personalized exchange involving a small number of trading partners at a local level. As the scope and size of exchange increased, a pattern of impersonal exchange developed, in which parties were constrained by institutions such as kinship ties, the exchange of hostages or codes of conduct. Over time, impersonal exchange with third-party enforcement arose as "the critical underpinning of successful modern economies involved in the complex contracting necessary for modern economic growth" (North 1990, 4). Since economic growth requires the development of increasingly sophisticated institutions, and in particular the development of efficient and low-cost contract enforcement mechanisms, North indeed sees in the absence of such mechanisms "the most important source of both historical stagnation and contemporary underdevelopment in the Third World" (North 1990, 54). Although he recognizes that complex exchange can take place by creating a voluntary system of third-party enforcement, he estimates the costs of such a system as prohibitive. In consequence, "[t]hird-party enforcement means the development of the state as a coercive force able to monitor property rights and enforce contracts effectively" (North 1990, 59).

The centrality of property rights and contract enforcement in NIE theory accounts for the current importance of business law on the law and development agenda. Whereas former law and development programs conceived of legal reform as encompassing all aspects of the law, the current movement explicitly emphasizes the fundamental character of laws regulating private economic relationships. NIE does not account, however, for the belief that institutional reform constitutes an efficient development tool. Indeed, for North himself, although "we know a good deal about the institutional foundations of successful development [...] [w]hat is still missing is how to get there" (North 2005, 28).

In order to find support for the use of legal reform for economic development, one has to turn to another leading figure in the development community, Peruvian economist Hernando de Soto. In 1989, de Soto published *The Other Path*, a study of Peru's informal economy that has proven a seminal work for law and development proponents. According to de Soto, the legal system is the main determinant for the difference in development that exists between the industrialized countries and developing economies, and legal reform should thus be the top priority of development programs.

De Soto's conclusions rest on a specific understanding of the nature of what he calls the "informal economy", i.e. those private enterprises operating outside the purview of formal law. According to him, the existence of an informal economy is directly related to the inefficiency of formal institutions: facing the choice between operating under a "bad law" having a negative on the functioning of their businesses and doing so informally, entrepreneurs choose on the basis of a rational evaluation of the relative costs and benefits of entering or exiting the official legal system. In consequence, "[t]he legal system so far seems to be the best explanation for the existence of informality" (de Soto 1989, 59). For de Soto, the institutions that "informals" generate to enable economic activity are more efficient than the State of the country in which they operate, but constitute inefficient substitutes for legally enforceable contracts. For example, the measures aiming at minimizing contractual risks and increasing compliance with contracts, such as investing in long-term friendship, investigating new partners, diversifying sources of supply and sales in order to spread risk, and relying on reputation-based constraints and private associations to enforce contracts, require time and effort that could be spent on more productive activities and thus lead to inefficiency. In addition, by creating barriers to entry for newcomers with no established reputation, they prevent firms from concluding possibly more advantageous bargains. In consequence, the key to both development and the suppression of informality thus consists in the adoption of a "good law" that informals would naturally embrace.

For de Soto, the best way to devise efficient laws consists in formalizing the informal norms in place. But, despite his influence in the development community, de Soto's advice concerning the formalization of informal norms has failed to become a standard policy recommendation. Rather than trusting informals to devise their own institutions in view of their particular needs and circumstances, the law and development agenda has taken the view that development requires implementing the "best practices" that have allowed for the development of industrialized economies. In the last 10 years, the World Bank has built a complex system to measure and compare the efficiency of diverse regulatory frameworks and identify the models that developing economies should emulate. As part of its Investment Climate strategy, which aims at turning developing economies into better places to invest, the World Bank has adopted a "benchmarking" approach that put developing economies in direct competition with each other to attract investment. For this purpose, the Bank uses data such as the results of Investment Climate Surveys, expert surveys conducted in the course of the Doing Business project, information on political and social conditions, and external evaluations such as the Credit Risk International, Institutional Investor, and World Economic Forum ratings, as "building blocks" to assess the quality of the legal institutions of specific countries.

The benchmarking approach is described in detail in the series of annual reports titled "Doing Business", which investigates the regulations that enhance or constrain business activity, with a view to comparing the business environments of different countries on the basis of new qualitative indicators used to analyze economic outcomes. As stated in the first report of the series (World Bank 2003, ix–x), the project has four objectives: motivating reform through country benchmarking, informing the design of reforms by backing indicators with an extensive description of regulations, enriching international initiatives on development effectiveness, and informing theory. Comparing regulation in poor and rich countries, the report makes clear that good regulation means less regulation for poor countries, whose generally heavier regulation leads businesses to operate in the informal economy. In contrast, rich countries present the "best practices in business regulation, meaning regulation that fulfills the task of essential controls of business without imposing an unnecessary burden" (World Bank 2003, xvi). There is, however, some good news for developing countries: "[m]any times what works in developed countries works well in developing countries, too, defying the often used saying, 'one size doesn't fit all'"(World Bank 2003, xviii). Furthermore, even though some "good practices" devised in rich countries might be hard to transfer to poorer ones, it remains possible to simplify the models used in rich countries to make them workable with less capacity and fewer resources.

The Issue of the Fit, Then and Now

The comeback of law and development has generally been eagerly welcomed, including in the academic community. This enthusiasm appears surprising when one considers the miserable results achieved by the legal transfers made during the first law and development movement and the disappointing results reached so far by the second, especially in the case of Eastern Europe (Hendley 1999). An important factor accounting for the popularity of the new movement undoubtedly resides with the theoretical and methodological tools used by its proponents in support of their claims. While the first law and development movement was based on little more than a "tacit set of assumptions" (Trubek and Galanter 1974, 1070) derived from evolutionary thinking which were rapidly called into question, the new movement benefits from well-developed theoretical arguments about the role of law in economic development. Moreover, by relying primarily on transaction-cost economics and cross-country macroeconomic data, the self-anointed experts in the field are in a position to frame the debate in terms that few people are trained in and comfortable using. As the quasi-exclusive preserve of economists or law-and-economics scholars, the law and development field has become almost immune to criticism from scholars of other disciplines. This leaves us to wonder whether, and to what extent, the new law and development movement has learned from the failure of its predecessor.

Lessons Learned?

The charges leveled against the reform programs of the 1960s and 1970s have been numerous and varied. Two of the main reasons said to account for the demise of the first law and development movement – i.e. the adequacy of law reform as an instrument of social change and the relationship between law and culture – are worth examining more closely.

Whereas the former question has aroused a large amount of interest in the academic community in the last 20 years, with many observers raising important doubts about the role actually played by law in economic development and the central role attributed to law reform in the development agenda, academics have shown little interest in the latter issue, i.e. the use of legal transfers, rather than "home-grown" laws, for development purposes. The little importance given to cultural issues seems particularly surprising in view of the central role played by the notion of culture in the elaboration of former development programs. Both colonial powers and the modernizers of the decolonization period insisted on the close relationship between local cultures and the law prevailing in developing countries. Despite disagreements on the length and endpoint of the transition process, all agreed that the institutions in place in the colonies were at worst barely legal, and at best of a fundamentally different nature than those found in the metropolis. As a product of immutable, "traditional" ways of living, local law was a remnant of an immemorial past that needed to be brushed aside for "modern" societies to emerge. In contrast, one would be hard pressed to find elaborate discussions of local cultures in the current law and development agenda.

The replacement of the customary/legal and modern/traditional dichotomies by the notions of formal and informal institutions is undoubtedly one of the major factors accounting for this situation. Contrary to customary law, which was said to be specific to "backwards" society, informal institutions are thought to exist in every setting. Legal reform is not meant to displace other forms of social control, but to expand the range of alternatives available to economic actors by providing attractive formal alternatives to existing informal solutions. This conceptualization of non-State modes of ordering as "informal" substitutes to formal law has important implications with respect to the process of transition from one mode of ordering to another. The notion that formal and informal institutions can substitute one another to fulfill the same social functions suggests a disconnection between informal norms and the cultural environment in which they emerge: far from being unique, informal institutions can be replaced by any other institution of similar or superior efficiency. Under this technological view of law, the legal transfers that were previously seen as a tool for state-building and fostering cultural change are thought of as a form of technical assistance with primarily economic effects. Following the idea that rational, well-informed people cannot fail to choose efficient institutions over ill-functioning ones, no resistance from the beneficiaries of reforms is contemplated.

By framing the issue in terms of "institutional change", the institutional perspective in fact suggests that, although it might be lengthy, the process of social change through law is ultimately unproblematic. Even though new formal institutions will not necessarily be valued at first by potential users, they will nevertheless create new trading opportunities and increasing competition, thus weakening the effectiveness of informal norms-based mechanisms. This will in turn have the effect of stimulating local demand for formal institutions, creating the conditions that will allow them to supplant community norms and networks. Social change, defined as the supplanting of "traditional" informal norms by new formal rules, will then result, following a series of rational choices made by individuals facing the consequences of changes in market conditions. By conceptualizing economic behavior as the result of rational cost–benefit calculations, the new law and development agenda assumes that individuals fully aware of the benefits of imported institutions cannot fail to prefer them to their informal alternatives. The new approach thus brings a simple answer to the question of legal effectiveness: the supply of more efficient and well-publicized laws will necessarily generate local demand for them. Thus, despite acknowledgements that "transplanting approaches uncritically from one country to another often leads to poor results" (World Bank 2002, 53–54) and that "the success of any policy intervention ultimately depends on the extent to which the chosen approach reflects a good fit with local institutional conditions" (World Bank 2002, 53), such warnings against uncritical transplants have very limited effects in practice. The overall result is a "build it and they will come" approach (Hendley 1999), very similar to the views held under the modernization paradigm and under which the question of "institutional fit" is a matter of education, professionalization, and access to justice, rather than "bottom-up" input and the customization of law.

The assumed connection between supply and local demand has proven elusive in practice. Many authors have noted that rule of law reforms have so far had at best mixed results and pointed to the need to consider more fully the issue of the kind of "fit" required between imported law and the receiving society. For example, a study of a sample of 49 countries found that legal transplants were more effective where they were responding to local demand for law, i.e. where they were adapted to local conditions and already familiar to the receiving population (Berkowitz, Pistor and Richard 2003a, 2003b). In contrast, for the World Bank, the initial absence of a demand for imported law is no impediment to the introduction of reforms. As noted by Stephenson (2000), legal transplants are expected to act like a Trojan horse and foster a "culture of legality" that will create the demand required for further reform. Although some resistance to change may be foreseen during the implementation process, the proper response to this challenge is not to customize the law, but to promote local demand by cultivating local "ownership" of and "commitment" to the reforms. For this purpose, particular attention should be paid to the political issues raised by legal and judicial reform. The challenges faced by would-be reformers include convincing decision-makers that reforms are necessary, dealing with opposition from diverse interest groups, "packaging" reforms so that they are credible and feasible, and mobilizing support and building capacity to implement the reforms. Information and education efforts are required to ensure that individuals will be able to assess the reforms at their true value and embrace them.

The emphasis put by the World Bank on the combination of "benchmarking" with "ownership" highlights the limits put on the participation that is ultimately expected from local actors. The use of benchmarking to assess local needs means that the problem of a country (a bad ranking), its objectives (a better ranking), and the solutions to its problems (better practices) can all be identified with a minimal degree of participation from local actors. The issues of participation and ownership thus emerge after problems have already been brought to light and solutions proposed by experts on the basis of available "knowledge". From this perspective, it becomes clear that the main objective of "participation" is not to ensure compatibility, but to provide ways to reduce politically motivated opposition to the reforms. As a result, considerable attention is devolved to the marketing of the reforms in order to diffuse opposition, descriptions of the reform process often reading like a battle between altruistic reform adherents and self-interested entrenched political interests impervious to the public good. In contrast, recommendations on how to assess and obtain the level of "institutional fit" between these practices and local conditions are at best extremely vague and at worst totally opaque. Although the Bank acknowledges that "the benefits from foreign experts who provide a comparative perspective should be fused with knowledge of the local legal community – knowledge of the language, social norms, and the socioeconomic factors underpinning the country's political structure and legal tradition" (World Bank Legal Vice presidency 2004, 13), specific recommendations as to the amount and type of "tailoring" allowed are conspicuously missing. Similarly, the way in which "participation" can be achieved also remains unclear, except for the fact that it can take place in the course of workshops or town meetings. The emphasis put on the solicitation of public views on proposed legislation, rather than prior to the elaboration of this very legislation, is quite telling and shows that the role played by local actors in the reform process consists in identifying potential obstacles to the implementation of reforms, and not to share their own views about which elements require reform and the form such reforms should take. The benchmarking technique ensures that the content of the reforms can be determined on the basis of pre-determined objectives defined in reference to the realities of Western industrialized economies. To the extent that local experts with insider information on local legal institutions have a role to play at the early stages of the reform process, this role is restricted to the evaluation of the degree of conformity of those institutions to the "best practices" already identified.

The notion that law is not a social product but an "institution" with a precise role to play in economic activity has allowed the new development agenda to present the issue of legal reform in culturally neutral terms. The emphasis put on the market and the regulation of private economic activity as agents of growth have made it even easier for reformers to eschew the issue of the "fit". Concentrating their efforts on areas of law considered fundamental to business activity, the new law and development experts see their field of intervention as a technical one, in which culture is unlikely to play a major role. The NIE foundation of the new movement allows effortless replication of the previous division of social life into cultural spheres, where "traditional cultures" can be tolerated on a limited and temporary basis, until "development" makes them vanish, and economic spheres, where the transition process from old to new modes of behavior is assumed to be unproblematic, as long as proper laws are put into place. Now as then, it seems that, as far as economic activity is concerned, very little, if any, room is left for cultural differences to express themselves.

Does Culture Matter?

Despite the low interest shown by policymakers in the impact of culture on the success of business law reforms, cultural explanations for "underdevelopment" have not only persisted since the colonial period, but have even gained prominence in the last 30 years. Former USAID official Lawrence Harrison is generally credited for the revival of interest in culture as an explanatory variable for differences in levels of economic development. In his famous 1985 book *Underdevelopment is a State of Mind*, re-edited in 2000, Harrison forcefully argued that culture was the primary cause of Latin America's underdevelopment (Harrison 2000a). About 10 years later, a widely read book by Samuel Huntington (1996) described the contemporary world as divided between a small number of civilizations based on enduring cultural differences, and underlined the increased salience of culture in the new global order. Following suit, a growing number of scholars and practitioners from diverse fields began to focus explicitly on the role of cultural values as obstacles to economic development, leading Harrison to note the articulation of a "new culture-centered paradigm of development" by "intellectual heirs" of thinkers such as Alexis de Tocqueville, Max Weber, and Edward Banfield (Harrison 2000b, xxi–xxii). Many of the authors associated with the so-called "new" paradigm have not shied away from taking categorical and controversial stances, such as saying that "culture makes almost all the difference" (Landes 2000), or, with respect to Africa more specifically, that the continent refuses to develop (Kabou 1991) or needs a cultural adjustment program (Etounga Manguellé 1991).

The conceptualization of culture as a potential obstacle to development presents developing countries with a dilemma: they either have to engage actively in the promotion of cultural change, or withdraw from the race to progress. Two major questions nevertheless remain, i.e. whether cultural change programs are efficient at all, and what role law can be expected to play in such a process.

The latter question raises a fundamental issue in legal theory and comparative law, i.e. the nature of the relationship between law and society. This issue has long been the subject of numerous and ongoing debates opposing, on the one hand, scholars seeing law as a mirror of society and its being closely dependent on it, and, on the other hand, those insisting on the autonomy of law and its capacity to change the society in which it operates. The notion of legal dependency, which states that legal institutions have a close relationship with the society in which they are born and grow, can be traced far back in history. Already in the eighteenth century, Montesquieu (1748) noted in his famous *L'esprit des Lois* that the laws "doivent être tellement propres au peuple pour lequel elles sont faites, que c'est un très grand hasard si celles d'une nation peuvent convenir à une autre".[5] The notion that specific local conditions call for specific laws has led to intense discussions among comparative lawyers about the possibility of transferring laws originating in one setting to another. At one end of the spectrum, hard tenants of the legal dependency position such as Pierre Legrand (2001) have argued that, since legal rules do not exist in a vacuum but receive their meaning from the society in which they are applied, the transplantation of a rule from one society to another necessarily involves a change in the meaning of the rule and, thus, in the rule itself. In consequence, legal transplants are not only difficult but absolutely impossible. At the opposite end, famous comparative law scholar Alan Watson (1993) relied on historical evidence about the pervasiveness of legal transfers to conclude that transplanting rules from one society to another is not only common, but also relatively easy. For Watson, the fact that law is rarely created specifically with a precise society in mind evidences that there is no need for a close relationship between law and society.

Many authors have taken the middle ground in the debate between legal dependency and legal autonomy, by suggesting that the success of legal transfers

---

5   Should be adapted in such a manner to the people for whom they are framed that it should be a great chance if those of one nation suit another.

might depend on the area of law concerned. For Otto Kahn-Freund (1974), e.g. legal transfers are sometimes more akin to the replacement of a carburetor than a kidney transplant; comparative lawyers should thus take care to distinguish between cases of "organic" and "mechanical" transfers before implementing new laws. Gunther Teubner (1998) for his part proposed the notion of "legal irritants" as a way to go beyond the simple opposition between law as a mirror image of society and legal autonomy. For Teubner, whereas law was formerly tied to society by its identity with it, it now ties up closely only with some of its areas and only on specific occasions. In the large areas of law that are now only "loosely coupled" with social processes, legal transfers are easier to accomplish. In those areas where law and social processes are tightly coupled, however, legal transfers have to face resistance which is external to the law and trigger a series of events through which "the external rule's meaning will be reconstructed and the internal context will undergo fundamental change" (Teubner 1998, 27).

For legal reformers, the notion that the success of transfers depends on the area targeted for legal reform is far from being new; the challenge is rather to identify whether a specific area is "tightly coupled" or "loosely coupled" to social processes, and, in the former case, whether reform is nevertheless possible and advisable. This issue has long been a subject of interest for legal sociologists interested in "legal cultures" and the impact of local cultures on legal phenomena. The term "legal culture", which is generally attributed to legal sociologist Lawrence Friedman, is generally defined in broad terms, as "those parts of general culture – customs, opinions, ways of doing and thinking – that bend social forces toward or away from the law and in particular ways" (Friedman 1975, 15). Most of the work done so far on legal cultures has related to the compatibility of transplanted laws with the culture of the legal professionals of the receiving societies, with particular attention devoted to the transfer of legal institutions across "legal families". Issues of relevance to the legal profession, such as the internal consistency of the legal system or the impact of the reform of the judicial process, have figured prominently in discussions of the compatibility between transferred laws and the receiving society. And yet, as noted by Pistor (1999), the fact that a reform is well considered by local legal professionals might signal that the particular interests of the legal profession have been addressed, but does not say much much about the needs and concerns of the intended end-users of the reform, including the business community.

Assessing the potential effects of law reform on economic activity entails broadening the scope of the inquiry to include broader questions about the compatibility of the imported norms with laypeople's legal cultures and practices. For this purpose, many authors have proposed to abandon traditional classifications of legal systems based on the notion of legal families in favor of alternative, more encompassing classificatory systems. Ugo Mattei (1997), e.g. has proposed a taxonomy in which legal systems are classified according to the type of norms – politics, law, philosophical/religious tradition – that play a leading role in behavior, and fall into three main categories: professional law, political law, and traditional law. Similarly, legal anthropologist Étienne Le Roy (1999), who sees law as resting on three distinct bases – *loi, coutume, habitus* – classifies legal systems according to the hierarchy they establish between these three types of norms. From this perspective, legal transfers could be contemplated between countries belonging to the same broad categories, but could hardly work where they involved a transition from one type of system or norm to another.

The idea that local legal cultures impact on the efficiency of transplanted laws has been particularly popular among specialists of Asia, and more particularly of Japanese law. Debates about the existence of a distinct Japanese legal culture started in the 1960s, when legal sociologist Tayekoshi Kawashima (1963) first identified a distinct national legal consciousness as accounting for the low litigation rates observable in Japan. Many authors subsequently interpreted Kawashima's work as an assertion that specific cultural values such as deference to authority and harmony have generated a general antipathy for law and distaste of litigation among Japanese people. Cultural differences are still widely invoked to account for the reluctance of Japanese entrepreneurs to document agreements, the brevity and lack of precision of their contracts, the flexibility observed in their application, and, more generally, the gap between the law in the books and the law in action. Cultural explanations are also popular among observers of sub-Saharan Africa in general. In line with the assertions of colonial law experts about the unity of African legal systems, most notably with respect to their common reliance on "the community principle" (Allott 1960a), numerous contemporary studies consider many sub-Saharan African settings as characterized by the pervasiveness of local practices emphasizing relational harmony within the community over the rights of individuals.

Despite their prevalence, bold assertions about the role of cultural factors on legal transfers are hard to justify on the basis of available information, which often consists in anecdotal evidence and "expert" views as to the legal culture of a specific community. Legal scholars are generally more interested in the potential consequences of the existence of relevant cultural differences on legal policy than on the precise identification of the "cultural traits" deemed incompatible with specific legal frameworks. This tendency is well illustrated by the treatment awarded to what has been called the "problem of ethnic minority market dominance" in the legal community. Even though sociologists and historians had long documented the presence, in many settings, of an ethnic minority group occupying a dominant economic position, as in the case of Chinese traders in Java (Geertz 1963) or the Kooroko community in Mali (Amselle 1971; 1977), the question only gained prominence in the legal community at the end of the 1990s, through the ambitious work of Amy Chua. Following a study of the consequences of the introduction of good governance reforms in settings where minority groups dominate the market, Chua argued that, since marketization and democratization reforms in such settings tend to favor different ethnic groups, their simultaneous introduction runs the risk of catalyzing ethnic tensions, leading to one of three non exclusive outcomes: an ethnically fuelled anti-market backlash, attempts at the elimination of the market-dominant minority, or a retreat from democracy (Chua 1998, 10). She thus recommended the adoption of "ethnically conscious" adjustments to the functioning of the market and the democratic process aiming at mitigating the potential negative consequences of ethnic disparities on the democratic process.

Chua's pragmatic recommendations rests on her skeptical attitude toward law-based cultural change programs: in her words, "while developing-country elites frequently urged their peoples to 'emulate the more successful minorities in their midst' and to become more 'diligent' and 'acquisitive', governmental 'cultural revolutions' – attempting to change culture and social norms by 'top-down' legal mandate – have not been famously successful" (Chua 2000, 343). For this reason, and while she recognizes the possibility that cultural factors may partly account for the existence of dominant minorities, she displays little interest in identifying the root causes of ethnic disparities or eliminating them. This has earned her a number of criticisms from advocates of cultural change. For Lan Cao, e.g. while dominance related to corrupt alliances and cronyism involve relatively uncontroversial measures, measures aimed at reducing minority wealth "derived from superiority in skill, hard work, and entrepreneurialism [...] are more difficult to justify" (Cao 2004, 1053–4). In the latter case, policies should be aimed at changing the attitudes and behaviors that impede economic growth among disadvantaged groups. In cases where a country is unwilling to invest in cultural change, "ethnically neutral" measures to enhance competition are preferable to policies based on affirmative action or positive discrimination. A similar argument is made by Davis, Trebilcock, and Heys (2001), for whom there is little justification for attempting to alter the ethnic composition of the commercial elites by promoting entrepreneurship among groups with different productive abilities and preferences. In other words, if and where culture matters, disadvantaged groups and developing countries face a difficult choice: either they embrace cultural change, or they accept to remain in a subordinate economic position.

In line with the low interest shown by legal scholars in the investigation of legal cultures, the legal community has failed to exhibit a high degree of openness to the diverse ways to assess cultures developed in other fields like cross-cultural psychology and management, in which quantitative data obtained through large-scale national and cross-national surveys are used to elaborate various frameworks – the most famous of which is arguably Hofstede's (1980) classification – for the classification of cultures along a certain number of characteristics.. Among the many "traits" identified by cross-cultural researchers as basic elements of cultures, individualism is the only one in which legal scholars have shown a significant interest. This is hardly surprising, since it has long been conventional wisdom to consider individualism as one of the main features distinguishing Western countries from other societies. Despite early and well-known warnings about the potential fallacy of the distinction between individualist and collectivist societies, such as Malinowski's remark that "the savage is neither an extreme 'collectivist' nor an intransigent 'individualist' – he is, like man in general, a mixture of both" (Malinowski 1951, 56), "modern" societies continue to be seen as more individualistic and confrontational than "traditional", collectivist ones. In the legal sphere, individualism has been hypothesized to impact on the resolution of disputes, with collectivist cultures, which are said to put more emphasis on people and relationships within large groups, being expected to be more reluctant to litigate than individualist cultures, whose members value self-reliance and are more likely to bring conflict to the open. For example, the increase of litigation rates in Kenya was once interpreted as an indication that the country was giving up "tribal" ways of solving disputes in favor of modern,ones (Abel 1979). Similarly, as noted by Haley (1978), rising litigation rates in post-war Japan were often seen as a sign of Japan's progress toward modernity. Conversely, it was generally believed that post-war Japan's "problem" of the low level of penetration of law into a social life, as evidenced by low litigation rates and the small size of the legal profession, would resolve itself following the overall modernization of Japanese society (Feldman 2007). More recently, in the 1980s and early 90s, the "litigation explosion" purportedly observable in the United States was sometimes described as the expression of a typically American cultural trait. Kritzer, e.g. ascribed differences in litigation patterns between England and the United States to cultural differences with respect to adversity, noting that "[t]he stereotypical images of the stoic English person and the complaining American are more than just stereotype" (Kritzer 1991, 422). A number of studies have also shown correlations between levels of individualism and attitudes toward conflict in general. Whereas individualistic cultures have been shown to emphasize the values of autonomy and competitiveness, the need for control and the importance of formal procedures and guidelines, collectivistic cultures have been said to prefer bargaining, mediation and other non confrontational and harmony-enhancing modes of dispute resolution favoring the preservation of relational harmony (Trubisky, Ting-Tommey and Lin 1991; Bierbrauer 1994; Sanders and Hamilton 1992). But it has also been convincingly argued that variations in litigation rates and dispute resolution preferences can be best explained by institutional factors, which make litigation a rational choice in Germany, but not in the Netherlands (Blankenburg 1994) or Japan (Haley 1978). Upham (2006) has similarly suggested that Japanese informal dispute resolution mechanisms do not derive from the so-called collectivist nature of Japanese society, but were rather specifically designed by the government to discourage parties from litigating.

The association of individualism with "modernity" – and economic development – and collectivism with tradition went basically unchallenged until the second part of the twentieth century, when the economic success of Japan, followed by a number of other Asian countries without a "modern legal consciousness", forced its reconsideration. The economic development of Asia during this period constituted a major impetus in the emergence of a new line of thinking seeking to revalorize the local ways of doing business condemned by the modernization logic. Arguments were developed that Japanese culture was a contributing, rather than inhibiting, factor in the country's economic development. This logic was subsequently extended to the cases of China and East Asia (more particularly Singapore, Taiwan, Hong Kong, and South Korea), whose common Confucian heritage and use of *guanxi* was identified as accounting for their success.

The rise of Asia constituted a challenge to a number of assumptions about the relationship between capitalism, individualism and Western "modern" law and questioned the centrality of Western law for economic success. The development of alternative forms of capitalism raised the possibility that different societies might take different paths to development, without having to embrace the cultural values and legal models of the West. By highlighting the role played by social relations in the formation and functioning of the market, research on Asian forms of capitalism also suggested that something else than individualism and the rule of law might account for the economic success of the West. It is in this context that the notion of "social capital" started to attract academic attention in the 1980s. Initially conceived by sociologists as the ability of individuals to secure resources by virtue of various social ties, it eventually became an attribute of communities conducive to a range of collective social goods such as lower corruption levels and better governance. Under the influence of well-known thinkers such as Francis Fukuyama and Robert Putnam, it rapidly rose to prominence to become a central concept in the investigation of the role of cultural beliefs and values in development. It was eventually consecrated by the World Bank as having "significant implications for enhancing the quality, effectiveness and sustainability of World Bank operations" (World Bank 2012b).

Although there is no clear consensus on what is comprised in the notion of social capital, most definitions combine two different elements that Putnam,

Leonardi and Nanetti (1993) call "networks of civic engagement" and "norms of reciprocity". The former aspect of social capital refers to the diverse organizations in which citizens can participate and be educated in the art of citizenship. The latter designates the norms, values, and virtues prevailing in a community that allow people to cooperate with each other, and constitutes an equivalent to the notion of "trust". Social capital perspectives hold that, since it allows people to cooperate more efficiently, trust can contribute significantly to market success.

The actual relationship between social capital and development is neither well understood nor well documented. Although resort to the term "capital" itself suggests that social capital constitutes an unqualified good positively correlated to development, the few studies that have attempted to provide evidence of this relationship have so far produced inconclusive and sometimes contradictory results. Two main hypotheses can be drawn to account for the inconclusiveness of the available evidence. The first one is that the relationship between development and social capital is not linear but obeys a more complex logic. Stiglitz (1999), e.g. has suggested that it is in fact closer to an inverted U-shape: by providing adequate mechanisms for contract enforcement and monitoring, networks of interpersonal relations allow for the initial development markets. As markets grow, however, the value of these relationships – and with it the value of social capital – declines, and formal legal institutions come to replace informal mechanisms. The second hypothesis is that social capital actually constitutes a qualitative, rather than quantitative, variable. In this case, societies would be expected to differ not in their "levels" of social capital but with respect to the "kind" of social capital they exhibit.

A number of scholars have adopted a qualitative definition of social capital and suggested that development implies not so much increasing a society's total stock of social capital, but moving from a social capital rooted in interpersonal relations within closed communities to a form of generalized trust more open to inter-group relationships. For Fukuyama (1995), e.g. societies can be classified in three broad categories: truly individualistic societies, such as Russia or some other post-communist countries, where both families and voluntary associations are weak; family-based societies, like China, Taiwan, and Hong Kong, where family bonds are elevated above other social loyalties, leading to a deficit of trust among unrelated people; and high-trust societies, such as the United States, Japan, and Korea, which exhibit a high degree of generalized trust and a rich network of voluntary associations. But, although the idea that there exist different kinds of social capital may be theoretically appealing, at the methodological level, it only compounds the problems already faced in the investigation of social capital as an asset to "stock". Conceived as a multi-faceted notion that designates quite different phenomena such as personalized and generalized trust, membership of associations, and personal values, that are difficult to measure in isolation and whose mode of influence on each other is far from clear, the notion of social capital has proved rather difficult to use as a research tool. In consequence, and even though they claim to establish a significant relationship between social capital and development, existing studies only show that there is a correlation between the indicators chosen to measure social capital and development, without establishing the existence of a direct causal connection or offering a credible explanation for this correlation (Portes and Landolt 2000). The relationship between legal institutions and trust also remains under investigated, with little and inconclusive evidence being currently available about the impact of formal institutions on levels of trust. In addition, the mere existence of a correlation would not necessarily mean that legal reform can be used successfully as a trust-building mechanism. While it is possible that law indeed has a role to play in fostering trust, it may also be that trust is an independent cultural phenomenon, the "bedrock of social and cultural habits" (Fukuyama 1995, 150) that allows legal institutions to function properly. In such a case, law could only provide a minimal basis for cooperation, in the hope that trust will end up arising from repeated interactions between distrustful individuals. In addition, even such an indirect effect on trust could prove quite limited in the case of societies with high levels of social polarization, which are correlated with low levels of trust.

In many respects, the notion of social capital does not seem so remote from more traditional "cultural approaches" linking development with the presence of particular traits such as individualism. The main difference may reside in the fact that social capital is even harder to define, measure and use in research than cultural traits. This suggests that what has allowed social capital to take over more traditional culture-based approaches has probably more to do with its rhetorical appeal than with its explanatory power. By positing that the same set of basic values underlies the operation of efficient markets and good governments, social capital provides an explicit link between market and good governance reforms, while accounting for the success of Asian capitalist countries and dominant ethnic minorities. By highlighting the commonalities between successful countries (i.e., their high levels of social capital) rather than their differences, social capital approaches provide a seemingly culturally neutral way to talk about interpersonal relationships: what distinguishes developed societies from developing ones is not their different social beliefs, but the kind of social capital they have developed. In practice, however, economic development remains a matter of being able to deal with others the "right way," i.e. on the basis of the "right" values. This has become evident in the aftermath of the 1997 financial crisis, which for many observers signaled the failure of Asian development models. Formerly celebrated forms of Asian capitalism came to be seen as manifestations of a crony capitalism that was at worst a contributing factor to the crisis, and at best a transitional form of capitalism bound to decline with greater integration within the global market. *Guanxi* and other types of reliance on closed networks of relationships were condemned as contributing to inefficient forms of segregation and corruption. Rather than an asset, they became equated with a cultural tradition ultimately incompatible with long-term development.

Despite their enduring popularity under different guises, culturalist arguments still lack the strong empirical support needed to properly address the question of the role of cultural barriers in business law reform. One important reason for this is undoubtedly the considerable methodological difficulties that the investigation of cultural hypotheses involves and the limitations of the available approaches. Studies that resort to cross-country comparisons are often unable to distinguish between correlation and causality, discarding the possibility that both variables have a common external cause. Consequently, the "proven" relationships have limited explanatory power. In contrast, ethnographic, "thick" descriptions of the culture of one or more societies provide a type of information that can be more usefully employed to develop hypotheses, but their usefulness is limited in a comparative context. More generally, studies that focus specifically on cultural explanations run the risk of underplaying the role of non-cultural factors in the genesis of legal and economic phenomena. From a comparative perspective, focusing on the existence of cultural differences can also emphasize contrasts and downplay similarities between groups and societies assumed to be culturally distinct, with the observed variations then being attributed to cultural differences.

In view of these drawbacks, one could expect to find strong and well-documented critiques of cultural arguments in the literature. But, although some have convincingly argued that cultural explanations cannot account for the existence of economically dominant ethnic minorities (Fafchamps 2004, 144) or Asian forms of capitalism (Dezalay and Garth 1997, 123), such demonstrations have overall been few, including among law and development experts, whose failure to display a significant interest in the role of culture in economic activity has left the question of the role of cultural barriers in business law reform largely unaddressed. As a result, most discussions about culture focus on the consequences of differences in entrepreneurship, wealth or "legal behavior", rather than their determinants.

The enduring belief of policymakers and many scholars that self-interest and rationality, rather than other values, dominate in the business sphere might account for the superficial treatment awarded to the question of the impact of culture on economic behavior throughout the different waves of legal reform that have taken place in developing countries. The dominant conception of economic decisions as the product of a universal form of human rationality entails that the development of an entrepreneurial spirit does not involve cultural change, but the replacement of cultural habits by universal decision-making processes. The spheres which are fundamental to economic development, such as contract and commercial law, are thus essentially "neutral," "technical" fields, in which legal models can be easily transferred. And yet, as the rest of this book will show, the idea that business transactions and relations are based on a form of universal rationality reflected in formal law has not been demonstrated. An adequate analysis of cultural factors in business law transfers as well as, more broadly, a proper understanding of business contracts, would require going beyond the opposition between cultural determinism and universal rationality, primitive and modern law, and formal and informal institutions, and exploring in more detail how and when culture actually impacts on business decisions. This would entail moving away from notions of culture as beliefs or as self-representation toward culture as expressed in action, and from values and attitudes toward behavior in real-life, rather than hypothetical, situations. From a methodological point of view, the challenge is to break from deductive approaches in which one looks for the intended consequence of a trait (whose presence is either "measured" or taken for granted), in favor of an inductive method in which relevant traits are first derived from observation, rather than chosen *a priori*. In other words, the real explanatory power of culture can only be brought to light by letting people express themselves freely, as complex beings for whom "cultural" and "economic" motives are tightly intertwined. The rest of this book constitutes a small, but arguably significant step in that direction.

Chapter 2

Re-assessing the Role of Culture in Business Contracts

Like its predecessors, the new law and development agenda holds that economic development requires economic actors operating in developing countries to abandon their current practices in favor of the "best" ways to do business in use in industrialized economies. It also shares their conviction that the process of transition to these best practices is essentially unproblematic. Unlike them, though, this conviction is not grounded on the assumed inexistence or inadequacy of customary norms regulating business transactions. In line with its functional orientation, the current agenda rather assumes that, in the absence of formal law, business transactions can, and generally do, take place through the support of functional, although sub-optimal, informal "institutions". From this perspective, legal transfers do not entail cultural change, but a simple, rational choice between less and more efficient institutional arrangements.

The reliance of policymakers on New Institutional Economics as a basis for the elaboration of the law and development agenda has had a profound impact on its understanding of the role of law in business transactions. The use of an economic conception of human decision-making as a "game" in which parties seek to maximize their benefits has led law and development proponents to conceptualize law primarily as a provider of "incentives" to cooperate. In consequence, the "efficiency" of these incentives has been considered both the primary factor accounting for the use or non-use of legal mechanisms, and the criterion according to which "formal" and "informal" alternatives are to be evaluated.

Such a functionalist conception of law as a set of state-backed sanctions carries significant consequences for the conceptualization of the relationships between informal and formal modes or ordering. From a functionalist perspective, formal and informal orders are basically considered as forming a "package" of "enforcement solutions" from which transactors choose in function of their respective estimated efficiency in each contemplated transaction. The result is the adoption of an "either/or" approach, in which formal and informal institutions work in parallel. The objective of law reform in developing countries is not to eliminate informal modes or ordering, but to turn those "substitutes" into "complements" of the formal legal order. From this perspective, law reform can hardly do any wrong, and, since it could do some good, it should be offered as an "alternative" to transactors in search of more efficient mechanisms.

This chapter examines the theoretical foundations of the current law and development agenda by looking at the role played by game theory and transaction cost economics in the conceptualization of informal enforcement mechanisms, and identifies some of the most important limitations of this approach as it is currently applied to the case of developing countries. It concludes with an exploration of potential alternative avenues for the study of business relations.

The Costs of Enforcing Contracts

The notion that the enforcement of contracts constitutes a "cost" that parties to business relationships seek to minimize has taken a strong hold in the study of business contracts. A review of current literature on informal enforcement mechanisms reveals the predominant role played by economists in this field of inquiry, with most of the existing literature accounting for the emergence and maintenance of informal mechanisms by pointing to their ability to lower the transaction costs incurred by parties for a certain transaction, in certain specific circumstances.

The basic notions of transaction cost economics (TCE) are generally held to have first emerged in the Ronald Coase (1937) paper on "The Nature of the Firm", before gaining influence under the leadership of Oliver E. Williamson (1975; 1985). In line with mainstream economic thinking, TCE assumes that individuals are rational and profit maximizing, and thus seek to minimize the costs they incur. Crucially, it also recognizes that market transactions are not costless. Before a transaction can even take place, some costs need to be incurred to find a potential partner, determine the appropriate price to pay, and negotiate and draft the terms of the exchange. Additional costs will also need to be incurred to monitor the other party and ensure that the contract will be enforced. All of these activities require expenses of time, energy and money.

Among the initial objectives of TCE, an important one was to account for the "rise of the firm" as an organizational form replacing the price system. It was hypothesized that firms emerge where the costs related to the "vertical integration" of a number of transactions are inferior to the costs of carrying the same transactions in the market. However, in the last 15 years or so, there has been a rise of interest in the variety of "hybrid" forms of governance forming the "swollen middle" (Hennart 1993) between hierarchies and markets. An important line of work concerns the impact of transaction costs on the type of formal contracts used by firms to govern their relationships. TCE has also been used to account for the existence of informal "governance structures" such as long-term relationships not governed by explicit contractual terms, and intra-community patterns of contracting. In one of the earliest and most influential works on informal modes of ordering, Robert Ellickson (1991) resorted to TCE to show that the Sasha County ranchers he observed could not only "achieve order without law", but that the norms to which they resorted were welfare-maximizing and superior to formal law. More recently, Lisa Bernstein has emerged as a leader in uncovering enforcement mechanisms used in specific merchant communities and analyzing their functioning in TCE terms.

Transaction cost economics accounts for people's choice between formal and informal enforcement mechanisms in terms of their relative efficiency. In Ellickson's words (1991, 282), "one reason people are frequently willing to ignore law is that they often possess more expeditious means for achieving order." Each option available to parties is said to have its own strengths and weaknesses, and to be "comparatively more adept – i.e. transaction-cost minimizing – than the others for a certain transaction" (Richman 2004, 2238). Assuming that "transactors allocate aspects of their relationships between the legal and extralegal realms in ways that seek to maximize the value of their transaction" (Bernstein 1996, 1788), the challenge then becomes to explain why and when specific informal mechanisms emerge and prevail over informal and formal alternatives, by assessing their respective transaction costs. In TCE, the costs of a specific transaction, and thus the "efficiency" of the particular "governance structure" on which it relies, depends on three main characteristics of the transaction: its level of asset specificity, the frequency with which it occurs, and the level of uncertainty associated with it. In consequence, the transaction costs associated with legal contracting and the relative efficiency of law compared to other enforcement options will vary in function of the type of transaction contemplated as well as the context in which it is to take place.

In recent years, a number of researchers have sought to define with more precision the circumstances in which people choose to "opt out" of the system and resort to informal alternatives by tying informal mechanisms to some inherent limitations of the legal system. Four main categories of "problems with the legal system" that can be solved by resorting to informal mechanisms emerge from this literature. The first – and most obvious – concerns the costs associated with the litigation process, which makes court use unattractive for claims falling below a certain threshold. The amounts at stake in a particular type of transaction will thus have an impact on the respective attractiveness of diverse mechanisms. For example, where a comparison of two tuna markets revealed that one relied on a simple *caveat emptor* norm, while the participants in the other had proceeded to creating a specialized "tuna court", it was hypothesized that the smaller size of the tuna sold in the former accounted for the simpler modes of resolution in place in this market (Feldman 2006).

The kind of remedies that courts can provide, and the speed at which they can intervene in the course of a dispute, is another point that limits the benefits associated with their use. Disputants who choose to litigate their claims may receive compensation some time after a breach has occurred, but will rarely be provided with adequate ways to deal with the more immediate consequences of breach on their lives and operations. Monetary compensation after the fact does not prevent plants from closing and clients from going elsewhere to find the goods they need. In many cases, preventing contractual problems and rapidly finding solutions to those problems that nevertheless occur are key to staying in business. Bernstein's (2001) conclusion that what participants in the cotton trade want is performance, not payment for non-performance, is undoubtedly valid in a number of trades.

The problem of costs could, to a certain extent, be resolved through the creation of cheaper enforcement mechanisms for the resolution of low-stake disputes. What is at issue as far as costs are concerned is not the nature of the legal system, but its accessibility. The same could be said, to a certain extent, about speed and remedies, although the reforms needed to address those issues would involve more serious reconsiderations of the principles underlying the functioning of the judicial system. The other two "problems" with the legal system seem fundamentally different in this respect, since they do not relate to the "efficiency" of courts – a problem to be addressed by institutional reform – but their "ultimate futility" (Richman 2004, 2332) when time comes to enforce certain types of agreements. A first case concerns contracts with high "bargaining" and drafting costs. In order to be enforceable by courts, a legal contract must contain provisions detailing contractual expectations whose compliance can be verified *ex post* by a third party. Where a contemplated transaction reaches a certain level of complexity, or where there is uncertainty surrounding the conditions in which obligations will have to be fulfilled, it may be too costly or even impossible for parties to negotiate and draft documents that appropriately describe the whole range of their obligations. For example, Woodruff's (1998) study of shoe production revealed that the quality of workmanship which is required from manufacturers in this industry can hardly be described in terms precise enough to allow the courts to determine whether returns from a retailer are legitimate or not. The second problem about the enforcement of contracts by courts is related to the difficulty of bringing certain facts under the consideration of the tribunal. Even where detailed contractual provisions can be drafted, they will be of little use to judges unless the relevant facts can be proven in court in case of dispute. This means that parties need to be informed of contractual breach soon enough to be able to sue at a time where the facts can still be verified by courts. For Bernstein, the distinction between observable and verifiable information is "one of the most important reasons [why] transactors allocate aspects of their agreement to the legal or extralegal realm" (Bernstein 1996, 1791). Where the outcomes of transactions depend on many conditions that cannot be directly observed by the other party or the legal system, as in the long-distance trade studied by Greif (1993) and Clay (1997), the creation of a coalition based on reputation is more efficient than adjudication. From this perspective, the Tsukiji tuna court is allowed to exist only because Tsukiji tuna are bought by small, family-owned enterprises that cut it immediately and resell it in the market. In contrast, Honolulu tuna are generally bought at auction by wholesalers who resell them to another buyer who will fillet them, eliminating the possibility of bringing the cut tuna to an adjudication session (Feldman 2006, 348).

TCE accounts for informal mechanisms by pointing to their ability to address the shortcomings of legal institutions in cases where the costs are too high for the amounts at stake, immediate compliance is highly preferable to delayed compensation, disputes involve complex notions that judges do not master and facts are hard to prove in the context of a trial. In order to better understand why informal mechanisms are said to contribute to contract enforcement without support from the state, it is necessary to have a closer look at how they are thought to operate.

The Contracting Game

Economists generally address the possibility that parties to a contract can self-enforce their agreement without recourse to law by combining TCE with insights from game theory. As its name suggests, game theory conceives of cooperative behavior as the result of a game played by two or more "players" seeking to maximize their own interest in the pursuit of economic ends. Players are expected to behave in a cooperative manner only as long as the returns from cooperation exceed the returns from defection.

Game theorists resort to different sorts of games to describe and predict different kinds of human behavior. Business dealings are generally said to correspond to the particular game known as the "prisoner's dilemma game". In this game, the best outcome for the two players is that neither of them cheats; however, the payoffs are set so that each player individually is better off cheating – violating contractual terms – than complying. In consequence, both will rationally choose to cheat, leading to a less favorable collective outcome. In order to induce cooperation, one must change the payoffs in order to make it rational to cooperate, e.g. by providing sufficiently severe sanctions for cheating. In legal terms, that entails making both the threat of legal action more credible and the consequences of legal action more costly for the defaulting party.

Another way to induce cooperation between parties to a prisoners' dilemma game is to require them to repeat the game – i.e. enter into other transactions with each other – in the future. In this case, parties acting in their own interest will be expected to take the "shadow of the future" into account and to cooperate for fear of later retaliation by the other. Repeating the game thus makes contracting self-enforcing through the threat of retaliation. The same logic can be extended to situations where interactions do not take place among the same individuals but among a pool of individuals. In such cases, the threat of retaliation can remain a deterrent against breach if information becomes known to potential future counterparts and these persons rely on it to refuse interaction. The key incentive here is the preservation of one's reputation, on which future interactions depend.

Discrete transactions, to the extent that they exist at all in the real world of business, form only a very tiny part of all the transactions that take place in everyday life. Most transactions do not take place instantaneously between anonymous partners, but in the course of a relationship of variable duration. Frequent and/or long-term interaction is said to play a positive role on enforcement because partners in such relationships are likely to refrain from cheating in order to maintain the relationship. The fear of losing the benefits of future exchange provides parties with an incentive to be honest. It must be noted, however, that ending a relationship constitutes a punishment only where switching is costly, i.e. where transactors cannot find equivalent goods from other sources without incurring additional costs. In other words, enforcement mechanisms based on the presence of a long-term relationship work only where there is some degree of "lock-in" in the relationship.

Lock-in can arise from many sources, including the structure of the market in which exchange takes place. For example, a buyer may be locked-in with particular vendors if no alternative supplier exists or can be found (at low cost) for the particular good they need. Lock-in can also derive from the specific investment made to screen potential partners, create the relationship, and make it run smoothly. Such investments are more likely to occur where parties derive benefits from familiarity with one another's needs, standards and modes of operation. In such cases, the significant costs to be incurred for similar efficiencies to be achieved with a new partner represent an important incentive for firms to comply and cooperate. Long-term relationships can also prevent opportunism in cases where information is asymmetrically distributed between the parties, opening the door to opportunistic exploitation of informational advantages. A classical example of this situation is the market for lemons described by Akerloff (1970), in which only sellers know the real value of the cars they offer for sale. Trade in used or non-standardized goods necessarily involves "a high degree of risk for the buyer in what precisely he buys, because no good is exactly like another he can buy from the same or a different seller or might have bought in the past" (Fanselow 1990, 252). In turn, sellers may be unable to sell their goods at their true value, since buyers are unable to tell the difference between higher- and lower-quality goods. Both parties can mitigate those disadvantages by establishing privileged relationships in which buyers agree to buy from the same sellers, who deliver them their best products in return. In such cases, lock-in occurs from the trust that develops between partners in the course of the relationships and the difficulty in locating trustworthy partners at low cost. For example, Geertz's (1978) now classical description of Moroccan bazaars showed that buyers find it rational to return to the sellers they know, even if others may offer better prices. Similar solutions can be expected to emerge where large quantities of products are sold in bulk, making the evaluation of the exact quantity provided problematic, and for commodities whose grading is a subjective process that the buyer cannot be expected to be able to carry in person, like in the cotton market described by Bernstein (2001).

The use of relationships as enforcement mechanisms presents one important limitation: it can only be effective where the relationship one threatens to terminate is valuable to the other party. In cases where one or both parties ascribe little value to the relationship in question, it may be necessary to attach additional adverse consequences to breach. Enforcement mechanisms based on reputation aim at doing so, by allowing reputation to replace relationships as a bond. It is then the prospect of losing a large range of profitable, reputation-dependent business relationships that deters transactors from breach. Two conditions are essential for such reputation mechanisms to work effectively. First, information about breach has to circulate easily among a group of people. Only then do their decisions about who to deal with stand to be affected. Secondly, threats of boycott have to be both credible and significant: information about past conduct has to reach people with the capacity to apply sanctions in case of breach.

A good proportion of the empirical work done on the operation of reputation mechanisms so far relates to relatively small and homogeneous groups of people corresponding to Ellickson's definition of a "close-knit community", i.e. "a social network whose members have credible and reciprocal prospects for the application of power against one another and a good supply of information on past and present internal events" (Ellickson 1991, 181). Close-knit communities are generally considered to be composed of a relatively small and homogeneous number of people who interact frequently with each other and share some common characteristics such as language, religion, ethnicity, or culture, such as the Orthodox Jews operating in the diamond trade (Bernstein 1992; Richman

2006), Chinese immigrants (Landa 1994) and medieval Mediterranean Maghribi traders (Greif 1989; 1993). A conventional wisdom in the literature is to contend that self-enforcement mechanisms are bound to break down outside the bounds of such homogeneous communities (Leeson 2006), with reputation bonds "generally assumed to be effective only within geographically concentrated, homogeneous groups who deal with each other in repeated transactions over the long run" (Bernstein 1992, 140). Aviram (2004) attempts to account for this situation by pointing to a "chicken and egg" paradox confronting private contract enforcement systems: they can be effective at enforcing behavior as long as they secure the cooperation of their members, but members will cooperate (i.e. comply with rules and apply sanctions) only as long as they receive benefits from membership. Since reputation-based systems that are in their infancy do not yet provide benefits to their members, reputation will work only as long as it affects interaction in some other network that provides such benefits. Consequently, private contract enforcement mechanisms tend to build on existing networks rather than emerge spontaneously.

Homogeneous, concentrated groups indeed share a feature that seems to allow reputation mechanisms to work particularly well. This feature, which Richman (2004) calls the "orthogonality principle", concerns their tendency to contain a large web of crosscutting relationships of different types. In such communities, "primary social bonds" – those bonds which have a direct impact on one's ability to share information and thus be successful in business – are intermingled with secondary social bonds, such as a shared culture, language, or religion. The fear of being "snubbed at the local club or suffer[ing] pangs of guilt during the Sunday sermon" (Charny 1990, 419) provides businesspeople with additional disincentives to break their contractual obligations. Social ties, such as those based on shared personal characteristics, thus provide groups based on these characteristics with a wider range of methods of influence than do groups connected only by business ties. The orthogonality principle also contributes to solving the "endgame problem" – the fact that reputation-based mechanisms restricted to business matters tend to become less efficient with time, as people approach retirement and the prospects of future transactions diminish. The intermingling of business and personal relationships allows reputation to be bequeathed to descendants remaining in the industry and to determine one's status in the community after retirement, providing additional incentives to cooperate.

To the extent that a pre-existing network is indeed necessary for the emergence of a reputation-based contractual regime, it seems that these conditions are not required for the maintenance of such a system. For instance, frequent interaction is not the only way by which information can be disseminated within a group. Early examples of alternative ways to share information include the system of private judges used in the Medieval Champagne fairs, whose function was to reduce the costliness of generating and communicating information, thus allowing traders to boycott dishonest merchants (Milgrom, North and Weingast 1990). Nowadays, technological tools can also provide means to efficiently convey up-to-date information to large groups of transactors, thus allowing the creation of mass markets based on reputational bonds. It could also be argued that membership in a formal professional association may be a substitute for membership in a community, even though the presence of some sense of community among members might allow sanctions to work better. Bernstein, e.g. notes that the World Federation of diamond traders has induced dealers to set up regional bourses with a high measure of social and ethnic homogeneity in order to take advantage of pre-existing social relationships (Bernstein 1992, 144). Similarly, West notes that the existence of geographical coalitions within Osaka's Dojima Rice Exchange meant that "[m]erchants within a particular coalition would be unlikely to cheat one another for fear of being barred from the coalition [and] merchants from other coalitions would think twice about cheating a member of another coalition for fear of mass reprisal" (West 2000, 2596).

One basic feature needed for community-based enforcement mechanisms to work is that members have to value membership enough to find threats of exclusion dissuasive. In other words, there needs to be some "barriers to exit" the group. In consequence, the members of such groups have to be selected according to the value they give (or are assumed to give) to the preservation of their reputation and membership. In the absence of "secondary social bonds", reputation-based mechanisms will be efficient only to the extent that exclusion threatens one's capacity to do business or make a profit. For example, McMillan and Woodruff (2000) mention the creation, in the US fish market, of a firm providing credit information to wholesalers on the Internet as an effective way to prevent non-payment by buyers by making them unable to find an uninformed wholesaler to buy from. The enforcement system devised in Mexico's footwear industry documented by Woodruff (1998) was also contingent on the presence of a captive set of partners. Once trade liberalization allowed Mexican retailers to buy from foreign firms, manufacturers lost their power to sanction them, leading to the collapse of the structured information system they had put into place. Similarly, Bernstein (1992) notes that threats of exclusion are taken seriously in the diamond trade because the central organization created by traders can rely on its tremendous market power to make it clear to new entrants that securing a steady supply of diamonds for their cutting centers depends on their respect of the established rules.

According to game theorists, although enforcement mechanisms based on long-term relationships or reputation constitute attractive options in the case of transactions which courts are unable to enforce or do so inefficiently, they also present some drawbacks that limit their overall efficiency. The major criticism addressed to these mechanisms is that they erect costly barriers to entry for outsiders. Because game-theory approaches rest on the basic belief that the availability of sanctions for defection influences how transactors choose their contracting partners, they assume that those who have non-legal mechanisms at their disposal will refrain from contracting with "outsiders" untouched by the operation of such mechanisms. By inciting firms to stick with their partners and making them reluctant to enter into new partnerships – even with lower-cost producers – these mechanisms thus make it difficult for new firms to attract customers. In the case of reputation mechanisms, the reluctance of members to deal with non-members also means that newcomers find it hard to establish the reputation of reliability and honesty necessary to become a member. New entrants who wish to acquire the personal characteristics needed for membership in a particular community may find it difficult and lengthy, if not altogether impossible.

The idea that "exclusion is the corollary of ongoing relationships" (Johnson, McMillan and Woodruff 2002, 259) – be they bilateral or reputation-based – suggests that, while non-legal mechanisms can constitute an efficient solution in industries in which transactions are difficult to enforce and that do not prohibitively suffer when entry is limited, their potential effect in other cases is to shelter inefficient incumbents to the detriment of more efficient entrants. By making customers reluctant to look for new suppliers, they ultimately prevent potentially productive firms and efficient firms from growing (Richman 2004, 2351), and limit the growth of the private sector. Legal institutions are thus required in order to encourage firms to try out new partners and allow new relationships to start and develop.

Studies of non-state, or private, enforcement mechanisms have allowed economists to make two major arguments, i.e. that complex economic transactions do not necessarily depend on the existence of a public legal system and that, under certain conditions, informal mechanisms are preferable to formal law for policing business relations. But, they have not entailed a reconsideration of the centrality of law for the functioning of markets. Despite the advantages they may have over formal legal dispute resolution in certain specific circumstances, informal mechanisms continue to be seen as limited substitutes to law and appropriate only in exceptional contexts. In Gomez's words, "examples of informality within modern and complex societies are seen as mere "pockets" of indigenousness" (Gomez 2008, 291), the presence of efficient legal institutions remaining essential to allow for a larger range of transactions to take place.

Enforcement Costs in Developing Countries

Even though they emerged primarily in response to concerns about the emergence and persistence of non-legal mechanisms in settings with "functional" legal systems, game-theoretical approaches to contracting have had a strong influence on economic development policies. Following a citation by Douglass North about the role of institutions, the 2002 *World Development Report* of the World Bank opens with a description of the "institutions" developed by eleventh-century North Africa Maghribi traders to support cross-border trade and solve problems similar to those faced a millennium later by people "striving to improve their well-being through market activity" (World Bank 2002, 3). Following suit, in the development literature, transactions taking place in developing economies are commonly being described as systems in which small groups of people linked through kinship, ethnic origin or previous dealings (World Bank 2003, 41) resort to informal contract enforcement mechanisms based on relationships or community sanctions.

Whereas the contract enforcement systems found in industrialized economies are accounted for in terms of their efficiency, one would be hard pressed to find any reference to the advantages offered by such mechanisms or their superiority over formal law in the development literature. As far as developing countries are concerned, the focus is put exclusively on the limitations of these substitutes for formal law. In other words, whereas Western firms are said to resort to relational mechanisms because of their superiority over efficient legal systems, firms in developing countries are assumed to compensate for the dysfunctional character of local legal systems by sticking to "old ways" of doing business for want of better, state-provided alternatives. The notion that relational mechanisms in fact form two quite different categories – those that develop or remain in place in spite of the presence of efficient legal institutions, and those whose existence is contingent on the inadequacy of the legal system – means that, as far as developing countries are concerned, the provision of new sanctions through law reform would allow transactors to contract with a wider range of partners than those currently touched by the operation of non-legal mechanisms, and enter into more efficient transactions.

The notion that the state legal orders of developing countries are dysfunctional has deeply colored the way in which enforcement matters have been investigated in those settings. Whereas researchers studying contract enforcement in industrialized economies resort to detailed, qualitative studies to record the presence and workings of non-legal mechanisms, the existence of such mechanisms in developing countries is generally taken for granted, as a necessary consequence of the assumed need for contractual assurance and inefficiency of the local legal systems. The tendency is then to look for mechanisms (such as patterns of repeat dealings of intra-community trade) to which theory ascribes an enforcement function, and then assume that they exist primarily because they serve enforcement purposes. Reliance on theory thus allows researchers to dispense with documenting the diverse reasons why such patterns could have emerged as well as their actual impact on the enforcement of contracts. A related assumption is that the "formal" and "informal" sectors form distinct communities whose members differ in terms of personal characteristics and enforcement preferences. A striking example of the association between "community membership", "informal enforcement" and "informality" figures in the questionnaire designed by the World Bank to investigate the practices of firms operating in the Senegalese "formal" and "informal sector": whereas formal firms were asked whether they had resorted to courts in the previous two years, informal firms were asked how many of their disputes were solved through the mediation of a "wise man" or "respected member of the community" during the same period (World Bank 2004a).

The theoretical focus put on social sanctions, ostracism, and shared norms has given birth to a general assumption that a good proportion of, if not all, trade in developing countries takes place among members of close-knit communities that secure access to specific enforcement mechanisms. But both those community-based sanctioning mechanisms and the patterns of intra-community contracting they are assumed to generate remain largely undocumented. On the one hand, the oft-cited, paradigmatic case of the eleventh-century Maghribi traders – who, as documented by Greif (1993, 241), ostracized cheaters until they compensated the injured – has recently been questioned by Edwards and Ogilvie (2011), who contend that the Maghribis made frequent and voluntary use of formal legal mechanisms and did not in fact enforce contracts through collective punishment by the entire community. The case of the Maghribis also appears somewhat exceptional when compared to contemporary data from developing countries. Marcel Fafchamps, arguably one of the scholars with the most experience in empirical work on contract enforcement, mentions that, in years of research in Africa, he has never come across such coalitions and forms of collective punishment (Fafchamps 2002, 2–3). Similarly, McMillan and Woodruff noted that Vietnamese firms are reluctant to sanction breaching partners (McMillan and Woodruff 1999, 638).

One could account for these failures to sanction by noting that parties who could in theory apply sanctions do not always have the incentives or capacity to do so in practice. In fact, real opportunities to apply sanctions seem to be conspicuously missing in many situations. Threats to sever a business relationship can only be credible where both parties have a real opportunity to deal with other, equivalent partners. In other cases, applying sanctions is a form of self-punishment. For example, Clay notes the strikingly infrequent use of collective punishment by Mexican California merchants, a phenomenon she attributes to the fact that, in many towns, there were often only one or a few active merchants. Since defaulting agents could not be replaced easily, merchants generally punished cheating by refusing to grant further credit, rather than refusing future interactions, and resorted to ostracism only where it was inexpensive to do so (Clay 1997, 203–4). Similarly, Hendley's case study of Russian firms suggests that firms with a finite customer base and direct competitors see insisting on timely payment from their customers as a sure road to bankruptcy. In consequence, they "go to virtually any length to avoid alienating the customer (even though the customer is in breach)" (Hendley 2001, 46). In such cases, the preservation of relationships might not be as much a way to make business run smoothly as the only way to remain in business. In practice, then, "retaliation is not as immediate or predictable as in the simple-repeated game story and therefore not as effective a sanction" (McMillan and Woodruff 1999, 638).

On the other hand, there are reasons to doubt that the business communities of developing countries indeed organize themselves around pre-existing, non-business groupings formed on the basis of ethnic, religious, or other personal characteristics. The available evidence rather suggests that factors such as ethnicity, family, and religion do not play a major role in the formation of business networks (Fafchamps 2001b, 204). The assumption that enforcement considerations are important determinants in decisions whether to contract with a particular partner also seems fundamentally problematic. If it were true, one would expect firms with more confidence that breach would be sanctioned efficiently to be more likely to try out new, unrelated partners. In a comparative study of six transition economies (Vietnam, Russia, Slovakia, Ukraine, Romania, Poland), reported by Johnson et al. (2002) and McMillan and Woodruff (2000), this hypothesis was tested by asking firms whether they would abandon their current long-term supplier for a new one offering a price 10 percent lower. Firms who perceived courts to be effective were 7 percent less likely to reject the deal with the new suppliers, leading the authors of the study to conclude that well-functioning courts lower switching costs and barriers to entry. It must be noted, though, that the firms surveyed were not particularly reluctant to switch partners: only 22 percent of the surveyed firms who did not trust courts, and 14 percent of those who did, totally rejected the better offer and said they would not even try out the cheaper partner. In other words, a large majority of firms were ready to initiate business relationships with new, unknown partners or even abandon their current partners for new ones, even though the justice systems in place were "very far from perfect" (Johnson et al. 2002, 261).

Many reasons other than the state of the legal system or the availability of alternative enforcement mechanisms may account for a firm's willingness or reluctance to try out or switch to new partners. Sticking with a current partner, even if another party offers cheaper prices, may be explained by the numerous non-price advantages deriving from existing relationships. In sectors where supply, demand, or prices are unstable and unpredictable, long-term relationships often provide a minimum level of security which compensates for the higher prices paid. In peasant marketplaces, e.g. one often finds "equilibrating relationships" (Plattner 1990) in which buyers and sellers trade some parts of the gains they could make by trading with other partners for some protection from the vagaries of the market. Similarly, Acheson's study of Maine's lobster market revealed that, due to seasonal variations in the availability of lobster combined with the inelasticity in demand, firms in the marketing chain choose to deal with "steady" customers and suppliers, under an informal understanding that they will do business with each other over the long run (Acheson 1990, 117). Long-term relationships may also be particularly advantageous where firms have a restricted access to credit facilities; since supplier credit is more likely to be offered to "good clients" who have established their reliability and whose orders reach a certain volume, firms with cash-flow problems may be tempted to stick with those suppliers from which they obtained favorable credit terms rather than "split" orders and risk losing their privileges.

In view of the numerous incentives that may make firms favor the maintenance of existing relationships over the creation of new ones, it may be suggested that legal reform is likely to make a contribution to economic development only where viable alternatives are , i.e. where market institutions already exist and switching costs are low. And yet, these circumstances are exactly those in which bilateral and reputation mechanisms, which are said to be based on "lock-in", are hypothesized to be ineffective. Where switching is a viable option, then, law reform probably does not contribute to breaking the barriers to entry erected by informal mechanisms as much as fill the void left by former informal mechanisms rendered ineffective by lower switching costs. Conversely, where (non enforcement-related) switching costs remain high, legal reform is unlikely have a major impact on firms' propensity to try out new partners.

Beyond Sanctions and Values: Exploring the Role of Trust

Transaction cost economics and game theory are based on the assumption that individuals are rational (although only "boundedly" so), self-interested, and opportunistic, and comply out of fear of punishment or in anticipation of rewards. In consequence, cooperation can only be achieved in the presence of an efficient set of "incentives" designed to ensure contractual compliance, which make it possible to "trust" the other party. In contrast, approaches emphasizing the importance of culture suggest that cooperation arises not because of sanctions, but because of particular values and norms that make people trust each other without the need for law. By making people reluctant to frame problems in legal terms and litigate their claims, cultural values may prevent law from affecting behavior. From this perspective, legal efficiency entails cultural changes that can be effected only in the long run.

One major difference between economic and cultural approaches concerns their conceptualization of the notion of trust. For economists, trust arises where incentives to cooperate are aligned in such as way as to make it reasonable to believe that the other party will refrain from behaving opportunistically. According to Williamson, this calculative form of trust, although fundamentally different from the trust that consists in expecting good behavior of others in spite of incentives to behave opportunistically (Williamson 1994, 97), is the only one that has a role to play in commercial relations (Williamson 1993, 486). In contrast, cultural approaches see non-calculative trust based on shared values as essential to the creation and maintenance of cooperative relationships. The challenge for policymakers is not to provide incentives to comply but to create the conditions required for the development of the kind of generalized trust needed for markets to function properly. Despite their differences, these two sets of theories share a feature that constitutes their most important limitation: their exclusive emphasis on a single explanatory variable – self-interest or culture – to account for the behavior of individuals. A more realistic account of contracting behavior would require departing both from cultural determinism and from the game-theory model, and accepting the possibility that the goals pursued by businesspeople are not restricted to either compliance with the norms applicable in their communities or the strict enforcement of their contracts.

Legal scholarship provides some interesting insights into this question. It has long revealed that business contracts are not necessarily seen as a list of obligations, but as relationships in which trust matters and allows the parties to benefit from the flexibility needed in business. Early classical studies have shown that businesspeople do not necessarily see failures to comply with the letter of a contract as a contractual breach requiring retaliation, but rather as problems to be solved in negotiations (Macaulay 1963; Beale and Dugdale 1975). Unfortunately, although this question is of fundamental importance for legal theory, its investigation has been severely limited by the reluctance of traditional legal scholars to engage in the empirical study of legal phenomena in general, and contracts in particular. Although many acknowledge Stewart Macaulay's 1963 study as a breakthrough, few have explored the path opened by this "preliminary study", with only a handful of contract law articles published attempting to build on his methodology (Korobkin 2002, 1040). Traditional legal scholars have paid considerably more attention to the proper judicial response to the disjunction between business law and practice, than to the investigation of the nature and extent of this disjunction. In legal scholarship, Macaulay's contribution is generally interpreted as evidence that contract theory has little to do with the realities of contracting, without further need to investigate this "fact".

Legal scholars nowadays basically agree that an overwhelming majority of transactions take place without the parties ever resorting to legal arguments or legal enforcement mechanisms. With all contract scholars being "relationalists", the debate is now over "the proper nature of *contract law*" (Scott 2000, 852). Legal scholars also share a tendency to see the gap between contract law and contracting practices as a relatively recent phenomenon that emerged as modes of production evolved in the course of the nineteenth and twentieth centuries. A standard account of the evolution of contracts would describe it as a three-stage process, going from community-based exchanges to impersonal market relations, and finally to complex, long-term relations between increasingly specialized firms (Gordon 1985, 577). Macneil's (1980, 10) famous notion of relational contract, e.g. builds on the idea that former "discrete" contracts are not appropriate to the regulation of exchanges in "a larger society of great complexity, involving extremely elaborate specializations, and subject to constant change." In the same way as legal realist arguments for the adoption of a more flexible, "neoclassical" approach to contracts were framed in terms of the need to adapt to the increasing complexity of economic life, arguments for further reform are often based on the idea that neoclassical approaches are not well-equipped to deal with new modes of production and exchange (Esser 1996).

Another point of agreement among legal scholars is that, even though law does not seem to play a central role in most real-life business relationships, it nonetheless "matters". Legal scholarship reveals two main conceptions about how law actually matters, and should matter in an ideal world. The first revolves around formalist ideas about the purpose of contract law. Scholars in this category conceive of contracts as sets of bargained-for promises made under the belief that they could, or could not, be enforced by courts. Assuming that businesspeople take legal rules into account when making contractual decisions and plans, including when determining the role that law will play in the course of their business relationships, they see the "gap" between law and business practices as the result of a rational choice made by transactors to operate under a dual set of rules, i.e. relationship-preserving, flexible, and self-enforceable norms applicable in the course of the relationships, and an explicit and legally enforceable set of rules appropriate when disputes escalate and relationships break down. For them, such a dual system can only be efficient to the extent that it erects clear boundaries between legally enforceable rules and flexible, self-enforced norms. Because of the neoclassical incorporation of vague customs and standards into the legal sphere, transactors are deprived of the security and predictability they need and forced to "opt-out" of the legal system, leading to "a mass exodus from the public enforcement regime" in favor of private legal regimes which "substitute clear, bright line rules and objective modes of interpretation for [...] vague rules and a subjective, contextualized approach to interpretation" (Scott 2004, 378). The solution is thus to return to formalist approaches which would allow courts to fulfill the tasks they are better suited for, i.e. the application of the clear rules the parties wished to be applicable at the end of their relationships.

Neoformalists face the opposition of "contextualist" scholars, for whom real-life contracts do not constitute sets of bargained-for promises made at a specific point in time, but result from an incremental process of negotiation and adjustment during which expectations emerge and are modified. Contextualists are of the view that, since businesspeople are unlikely to wish to pursue legal sanctions in the event of a breach of contract, they also are likely to give little consideration to the enforceable character of their agreement or the applicable legal rules (Collins 1999, 123). The actual content of legal rules is unlikely to make a difference in practice beyond its impact on the results reached by courts in litigated cases. In consequence, such rules should not aim at being predictable, but at generating fair decisions in litigated cases. This requires departing from formalism and applying flexible rules taking all contextual and individual circumstances into account. Proponents of an increased contextualization of law contend that traditional conceptions of contracts are not compatible with the empirical reality of contracting. They interpret the gap as the result of the persistent reliance of legal theorists on a classical, promise-based conception of contract, and argue for its replacement with a new concept more in line with the realities of contractual relationships.

Ian Macneil's relational contract theory arguably constitutes the most well known attempt to develop a non-promise-based theory of contract. The major insight of Macneil's theory is that "contracts" are indistinguishable from exchange relations. Rather than the transactions contemplated by classical contract theory, contracts can be better described as forming a continuum going from almost-discrete transactions to highly relational contracts. On the basis of the observation of the "behavioral patterns" exhibited by parties to contracts at different points of the continuum, Macneil asserts that 10 "common contract norms" apply to all contracts, although to a varying extent depending on the position of the contract on the relational continuum. Although Macneil has taken care to emphasize the descriptive, rather than prescriptive, nature of his theory (Macneil 2000, 899), this has not prevented other scholars from highlighting the normative implications of a relational understanding of contracts. For Feinman (2000), e.g. law should differentiate between contracts according to their relational context. Collins also argues for "recontextualizing contractual agreements" by examining them in their "embedded context of a business relation and market conventions" (Collins 1999, 356).

One common point between "formalists" and "contextualists" is their general lack of interest in empirical research. Leaving most of the empirical ground to "law-and-economics" researchers, legal scholars generally base their recommendations on assumptions about the role(s) played by law in contractual matters as well as their own beliefs about the proper purpose of contract law. The historical and normative approaches they take say little about the actual role of law in business relationships, in both industrialized and developing economies. For a fuller treatment of the question of the nature of "trust" and empirical investigations of its role in cooperative relationships, one has to turn to some important contributions made in the field of economic sociology.

In contrast to economists, for whom cooperation depends on the presence of incentives not to cheat, economic sociologists focus on the impact of the social context in which business relationships take place on the behavior of parties to such relationships. From this perspective, "trust" is not primarily a matter of sanctions or cultural values, but can be better conceived as the product of ongoing social relations. In order to understand the role it plays in contracting, it is thus necessary to acknowledge the profound "embeddedness" of economic relations into the overall social structure.

The notion of embeddedness, which is often traced back to Karl Polanyi (1957), was revitalized in 1985 by Mark Granovetter, in what became the foundational text of New Economic Sociology. In "Economic Action and Social Structure: The Problem of Embeddedness", Granovetter criticizes both "undersocialized" and "oversocialized" accounts of economic action for their neglect of the ongoing structures of social relations in which economic transactions take place. According to him,

> [a]ctors do not behave or decide as atoms outside a social context, nor do they adhere slavishly to a script written for them by the particular intersection of social categories that they happen to occupy. Their attempts at purposive action are instead embedded in concrete, ongoing systems of social relations (Granovetter 1985, 487).

During the 20 years following the publication of Granovetter's piece, the notion of embeddedness has not only taken deep root in economic sociology but has rapidly spread to a number of other sub-fields and social sciences disciplines, including management and economic geography. A significant amount of research has studied the way in which social relationships between exchange partners affect economic action, including the ways in which firms initiate and manage their business relations. Partners who believe that the other party can be trusted regardless of their "incentives" to cooperate have been said to dispense with detailed contractual clauses to plan, monitor, and enforce agreements, to rely on one another's word and to solve disputes amicably (Claro, Hagellar and Omta 2003, 706). In such circumstances, business relations are essentially "non contractual", with law playing a very minor role in their governance.

The Emergence of Trust and Contract

The idea that trust is the product of social relations suggests that people who know each other before entering into a business transaction are more likely to trust each other. The same can be said where parties do not know each other personally but belong to a network in which they are connected through the intermediary of a third party. It is easy to understand how past relationships can contribute to the emergence of trust between two people. Past, repeated experience with a person improves one's knowledge of the person, builds one's confidence in the other's tendency to cooperate, and increases the potential for future interaction. A shared past also strengthens personal relationships between organizations, trust increasing as their attitudes, values and goals become more similar (Kamann, Snidjers, Tazelaar and Welling 2006). From this perspective, trust is thus a cumulative process that involves escalation from small to more significant forms of exchange. In sum, in the words of social network theorist Ronald Burt, "trust is a correlate of relationship strength" (Burt 2001, 33), which itself depends on the sequence of economic exchange between two parties.

The question then becomes one of defining and measuring what makes a relationship strong enough to be governed by trust. The duration of a relationship – by far the aspect of relationships that is the easiest to measure and quantify, e.g. by resorting to simple variables such as the number of years parties have dealt together – is the dimension of embeddedness, which has received the most attention so far. A number of studies have attempted to assess the effect of relationship duration on diverse aspects of business relations, such as the overall satisfaction of a buyer with a supplier (Poppo and Zenger 2002), levels of conformity to industry norms (Heide and Stump 1995), and the occurrence of contractual problems (Rooks, Raub and Tazellar 2006; Kamann et al. 2006). Yet, resorting to duration as a determinant of trust presents important limitations, including the impossibility to distinguish between cases where relationships are maintained because partners share a positive past experience and trust each other, and those where parties keep on working together for lack of adequate alternatives. Presuppositions of a direct connection between the length of a relationship, which reveal a tendency to assume intimacy in enduring relationships (Yngvesson 1985, 625) and "conflate the duration of a market relationship with the degree to which it is called 'social'" (Krippner 2001, 785), make one unable to capture those cases where trust is able to develop independently of the length of the relationship.

A more accurate understanding of the development of trust involves paying attention to the qualitative dimension of relationships. Contractual business relationships often form between people who share other kinds of ties, and it has been argued that those ties reinforce relationships and impact on cooperation. For example, borrowers that rely on a specific bank for additional services such as financial planning or the issuance of personal credit cards have been shown to be able to secure capital at more favorable interest rates than others (Uzzi and Gillespie 1999, 456). Similarly, DiMaggio and Lough's (1998) investigation of people's use of social ties in the process of purchasing cars, homes, and legal and home maintenance services, revealed that a substantial percentage of major transactions took place between friends, relatives, and acquaintances, and that people who transact with friends report greater satisfaction.

It has also been noted that continuing economic relations often lead to the development of personal ties that have an impact on how partners cooperate in economic exchange. Darr's (2007) ethnographic study of the relationships between buyers and sellers in the electronic components industry well illustrates this phenomenon, by showing how, in an industry where competition between sellers is fierce and clients can easily switch from one seller to another, sellers manage to keep their clients and gain new ones by visiting them regularly, giving samples, making suggestions, and providing advice, with a view to creating a tacit, moral obligation in buyers to sustain the relationship. In addition, even though they could benefit from low switching costs, buyers do not search extensively for partners before deciding on a sale but repeatedly activate existing relationships and are reluctant to break them. They contribute to the "mutual weaving of obligations" which allow sellers to reduce their dependence on buyers, while making life easier for buyers who can rely on their preferred sellers' expertise.

It is hardly surprising to see people having different expectations concerning strangers and people with whom they have built a relationship. It is commonsense to expect the people "one knows" to treat one more fairly and generously than unrelated parties. An interesting question concerns the "personal knowledge" threshold required for such expectations to arise: is it necessary to have a direct relationship with someone to consider this person as someone we can trust? It seems that expectations of fair treatment can arise between parties who do not know each other, if an intermediary they both trust introduces them. Brian Uzzi

(1996) provided a fascinating account of this process in his influential study of New York apparel firms. He showed that those firms, along with market ties, maintain with some of their partners "special relationships" that he calls "embedded ties". These ties, which are characterized by a unique "logic of exchange" in which firms cultivate long-term relationships rather than pursuing short-term gains, rarely originate from anonymous market ties. Rather, they tend to be established on the basis of previous ties between the parties or through third-party referrals. In the latter case, expectations arising from pre-existing relations between the referrer and two members of his network are applied to a new relationship between the referred partner and the referee. Conversely, the creation of social ties with members of one partner's network may also contribute to the creation of shared expectations between partners. For example, another study by Uzzi shows that informal social events involving bankers and borrowers as well as other persons, such as their respective spouses and children, on which parties confidentially rely for perceptions of character and trustworthiness, create social attachments which promote expectations of trust in the exchanges (Uzzi 1999, 488). Similarly, experiments have shown that belonging to the same sports club as a car dealer increases one's propensity to buy a car from the dealer in question (Buskens 2002).

By modifying expectations concerning the behavior of potential partners, social relationships can foster cooperation even in the absence of sanctioning devices. This has led many authors to point to the "competitive advantages" that firms can expect to gain by cultivating "embedded ties" rather than arm's-length, market relationships. Their main argument is that, by infusing business relationships with non-competitive values seen as uncharacteristic of market relationships, embedded ties allow firms to dispense with the formal contracting process, lower their monitoring costs, avoid the difficulty of planning for hard-to-predict contingencies and achieve efficiencies which are difficult to emulate in arm's-length ties (Dyer and Singh 1998; Uzzi 1997). The fact that problems are dealt with in real time during the production process, rather than in advance or in the course of a legal dispute, also represents economies of time and minimizes the impact on business activities. In addition, by allowing firms to easily adjust their agreements in response to unforeseen conditions, trust makes them more responsive to change, a key advantage in industries that place a high premium on innovation and customization (Powell 1990).

As the notion of "competitive advantage" suggests, research on embedded ties often adopts a functional perspective, from which social ties are created and/or activated because they allow a specific business relationship to be governed by a distinct "non-contractual logic" of exchange emphasizing cooperation. In their absence, parties have to revert to market forms of exchange – "one-shot deals" characterized by the lack of reciprocity between exchange partners, their pursuit of their economic self-interest, and cool relationships lacking social content – and resort to detailed contractual provisions to ensure compliance. As the opposition between the "logic of embeddedness" and the "contractual logic" suggests, trust and contract are seen as substitutes, "with contract leading to less trust, and trust leading to decreased contract completeness" (Woolthuis, Hillebrand and Nooteboom 2005, 818). This entails that legal contracts play at best an insignificant role in transactions between embedded partners, and may even have negative impacts on trust and cooperation. Resorting to contractual safeguards in embedded relationships is not only unnecessary, but also runs the risk, in Macaulay's terms, of turning "a cooperative venture into an antagonistic horse trade" (Macaulay 1963, 15).

The notion that "embedded ties" provide firms with advantages difficult to obtain in the context of market relationships regulated by contracts has not been free from criticism. It has been argued that, along with their functionality, embedded ties also present constraining aspects that limit their advantages (Podolny and Page 1998). For example, reliance on a small number of privileged ties may reduce the flow of new information to which a firm has access, with the possible consequences of cutting it off from other opportunities, insulating it from market demands, and stifling innovation (Uzzi 1997, 58–9). Clinging to trusted people for advice might also cut firms off from broader sources of useful feedback (Mizruchi and Brewster Stearns 2001). More importantly, personal feelings or social norms inhering in embedded relationships may conflict with the economic imperatives faced by firms. This is the "paradox of embeddedness" identified by Uzzi: feelings of obligation and friendship may lead stronger firms to "dedicate resources to weaker members at a rate that outpaces their capacity to rejuvenate their own resources"; in case of conflict, negative emotions of spite and revenge may also lead to feuds diverting the firm from the demands of the market (Uzzi 1997, 59). Thus, even though social relations can have positive effects on trust and performance, this is true only up to a certain threshold of "overembeddedness" after which the disadvantages of embeddedness exceed its benefits (Uzzi 1996; Dulsrud and Gronhaug 2007).

Business Ties in Developing Countries: Embedded or Overembedded?

By documenting the existence of business relationships that correspond neither to the economic model of market exchange, nor to the notion of community-based, social relationships, embeddedness research allows for the exploration of a middle way between economic and cultural perspectives on contract enforcement. Its main contribution has been to draw attention to the role that social relationships play in the creation of trust and the initiation and management of business transactions. Under this approach, the classical distinction between commercial transactions depending on the presence of sanctions and non commercial forms of exchange based on shared values has been superseded by a distinction between "arm's length/legal" and "embedded/trust-based" transactions. Borrowing Zelizer's (2005) terminology, the result is the replacement of a "nothing but" economics approach by a "hostile worlds" perspective, in which embedded exchanges are built in opposition to the market model and exclude the use of legal enforcement mechanisms.

In the development context, the view that embedded exchanges constitute an efficient, alternative to market/contract-based transactions has led to the suggestion that the creation of "clusters" of firms can provide a solid basis for economic growth and constitute "a useful model" for the industrialization of developing countries (Meagher 2006, 473). But despite this emphasis on the role of networks in economic activity, economic sociology has made a limited contribution to the study of the networks of business relations in place in developing countries. In fact, as noted by Meagher (2005; 2007), current research on this matter is characterized by a shared conviction that the networks in operation in developing countries are "overembedded" and thus do not form an adequate basis for embedded forms of exchange. Existing networks are said to be unable to deal with the problem of "uncontrolled solidarity" (Granovetter 1995, 1370) and to let the presence of "exacerbated" sentiments of solidarity turn promising firms into "welfare hotels" (Portes and Sensenbrenner 1993, 1339) or relief organizations. African networks, more particularly, tend to be seen as a *gangue communautaire*, a sort of communitarian quagmire, preventing managers from making rational economic decisions and firms from separating from households and other social units (Labazée 1995, 143). In consequence, it is thought necessary to break existing networks and replace them with ones where dysfunctional, redistributive community values do not operate (Portes and Sensenbrenner 1993).

It must be noted that the widespread characterization of developing countries' networks as overembedded, and the resulting lack of interest in their potential roles in economic development, does not appear to derive from a deep understanding of the composition and functions played by those networks. It might better be attributed, on the one hand, to the quasi-exclusive focus put by economic sociologists on the structure of the networks in which trust is built, to the detriment of the content of the ties forming those networks and the processes through which such ties are formed and trust emerges in the course of relationships, and, on the other hand, on the dearth of available data on the composition of developing countries' networks and the variables at play in their formation. Taking for granted that the business networks existing in developing countries originate from the clan-based, ethnic or religious communities to which businesspeople belong, researchers have concluded that such networks are necessarily overembedded and form an inadequate basis for the development of embedded ties similar to those found in industrialized economies. They also have failed to fully consider important insights about the formation and persistence of networks and embedded ties. For example, the notion, now well accepted in economic sociology (Baker 1990; Podolny and Page 1998), that firms may manipulate network ties strategically in order to limit their dependence by developing privileged ties with the sources of this dependence, has failed to find resonance in the case of developing countries. Moreover, the little available data hardly supports the hypothesis that business networks are based on "strong" ties originating in "communities" based on identity markers. Some cases have been documented that show that firms in developing countries can and do escape the demands of uncontrolled solidarity by building business relationships with outsiders with whom they can adopt more competitive practices, suggesting that at least some firms are in a position to build business networks distinct from the "communities" to which they belong, without having their membership called into question. It also seems clear that intra-community patterns of contracting do not necessarily result from a series of choices to deal with trustworthy partners, but from other factors, including the impossibility for firms operating in developing countries to prove themselves trustworthy to outsiders.

Assessing the capacity of formal law to impact on the practices of firms operating in developing countries would require a better understanding of how business contracts are formed and enforced in developing countries. This would entail going beyond the notion that "closed-knit communities" enforce contracts and look more closely at the role actually played by trading or social groups and norms in contracting practices. In this respect, "embeddedness" research's main advantage over approaches based on TCE concerns its attention to the variety of trust-related efficiencies one can achieve through the creation of embedded ties. Its relevance has been limited, however, by the difficulty it has, clearly apparent in the work of economic sociologists, in breaking from an economic view focusing on the role of sanctions.

A clearer departure from the game-theory model would be required in order to shift the focus from the deterring and enforcement functions of networks to the other functions they may serve, and acknowledge the possibility that contract enforcement is not the primary concern of businesspeople. Indeed, the high degree of flexibility that characterizes embedded ties suggests that parties to such contracts are not concerned with limiting the frequency of contractual breach as much as with finding mutually beneficial ways to deal with such breaches. Non-compliance with the terms of a contract is more likely to be seen as a problem to be solved in negotiations rather than instances of contractual breach requiring retaliations. Conversely, insisting on strict compliance entails performing one's side of the bargain to the letter and losing the "flexibility" needed in business. In the case of developing countries, where firms face tight financial constraints and the business environment is highly uncertain, the ties that develop between firms cooperating over a long period of time may be of particular importance in devising ways to manage crises. In addition, transacting on an ongoing basis allows problems occurring at one point to be fixed later in the course of the relationship. In other words, transactors may agree to cope with breach at one point in time, under the understanding that the other party will eventually make up for the breach. Flexibility can also by itself constitute a form of insurance in which a party refrains from retaliating after a breach under the understanding that the other party will reciprocate further down the road.

An accurate understanding of contract enforcement in developing countries requires going beyond the study of firms' contracting patterns and taking a look at the wide range of factors likely to have an impact on contractual dealings. In particular, more work is needed on the notion of contractual flexibility, its relevance in the context of developing countries, and its relationship to enforcement and compliance. For example, it has been suggested that where strict compliance is difficult because of external factors, applying sanctions in all cases of breach, including involuntary breach, would entail ending a wide range of profitable relationships, with no deterrent effect on the remaining partners. In such circumstances, renegotiation is likely to constitute the standard response to breach, sanctions being restricted to cases of "faulty" breach (McMillan and Woodruff 1999; Fafchamps 2004). From this perspective, continuing business relations are not meant to ensure compliance, but allow cases of non-compliance to be dealt with in a cooperative manner.

The kind and degree of contractual assurance actually sought by firms operating in developing countries, and how they manage or fail to obtain such assurance, remain largely unknown to this day. Many questions are still unanswered about the trading patterns in place in developing countries, the factors influencing the selection of business partners, the informal mechanisms used by businesses, and the reasons for preferring them to legal alternatives. The rest of this book is devoted to the examination of those questions.

Chapter 3

Law, Business and the "Investment Climate" in Dakar

The field study described in the rest of this book was aimed at filling some of the current gaps of our understanding of the role of law in business matters in sub-Saharan African developing countries, for which very little data is available. The study was conducted in 2006 in Senegal and involved the conducting of in-depth interviews with a small sample of small- and medium-sized enterprises operating in the city of Dakar. In selecting the participants in the study, the objective was not to create a sample that represented a larger population, but to gather accounts that were both sufficiently different to be held to represent an important proportion of the range of cases that could be observed, and similar enough to lend themselves to comparison (Sandelowski 1995, 180). In total, 30 representatives of SMEs were interviewed. Informal meetings were also held with business lawyers, the heads of two business associations, representatives of two organizations working with SMEs, representatives of the Dakar arbitration and mediation center, the director of a financial institution regularly dealing with SMEs, an employee of a debt collection agency, and two academics from departments of management and economics.

The main objective of the interviews was to identify the types of contract enforcement problems faced by SMEs, the sources of those problems, the methods used to solve them, and the reasons accounting for the use or non-use of courts for this purpose. The SMEs interviewed were chosen in order to maximize variation with respect to two sets of variables. First, the importance of variables related to the type of transaction between the parties and the industry in which they operate on the evolution of their disputes was explored by including firms from the manufacturing, trade and service sectors, and representing a good variety of industries within each of these sectors. Twelve participants were involved in the import, installation and servicing (where applicable) of goods as diverse as IT equipment, auto parts, shoes, textiles, clothing, stationery, food, automotive products and biomedical supplies. Three were providers of goods and/or services in the construction industry. Four offered specialized training or consulting services. Manufacturing firms were almost equally split between "traditional" manufacturers (furniture, clothing, hardware) and firms involved in more high-tech industries (chemicals, plastic elements, IT). Secondly, some demographic variation was sought after in order to explore the role of "cultural" traits on disputing behavior. The diversity of the Dakar business community was reflected by including in the sample people from diverse ethnic origins, including a small number of people born outside of Senegal. No attempt was made to screen participants with respect to other demographic characteristics such as gender, religious affiliation, age and level of education. The participants' profiles nonetheless proved quite varied on all those dimensions, except with respect to gender, with only one interviewee being a woman. Although no specific question was asked regarding the participants' religious beliefs, ethnic origin, or level of education, in many cases, relevant information was either given in the course of the conversation or could be deducted from other indications such as the display of signs indicative of religious affiliation.

The constitution of an adequate sample was subject to many practical constraints. One constraint concerned the difficulty in identifying with any certainty the firms forming the research population. No reliable listing of Dakar firms was available at the time of the study. The document closest to such a listing was the directory published by the Chamber of Commerce and Industry of Dakar (CCIAD), which contained the names of the CCIAD's members as well as some information on their sectors of activity, their owners and, in some cases, their size. The information, which was provided by the firms themselves, was generally very minimal and often outdated. In addition, the CCIAD's membership represents only a portion of the firms operating in Dakar.

Even if an official listing had been available, it would in all likelihood have been of little help in securing appointments with potential informants. The best, and often only way, to convince potential participants to agree to an interview was to make contact through a local intermediary or introduce oneself as referred by a common acquaintance, in which cases positive response rates were very high. In consequence, sampling first began with accessible sites, and built on the connections made with the initial participants. The limitations associated with convenience and snowball samplings were reduced by multiplying the number of "entry doors", i.e. three business associations with different orientations, two organizations offering services to SMEs, and personal contacts. Those who agreed to take part in the study were asked to provide the names of people who might be interested in doing the same.

An accurate understanding of the behavior exhibited by Dakar SMEs with respect to business disputes requires having a proper grasp of their situation, including the constraints they face when making decisions. For this purpose, the business environment in which Dakar SMEs operate will first be described through a brief account of the evolution of Dakar's business community and legal system. The data gathered in Dakar will then be presented, beginning with a presentation of Dakar's business environment as the interviewees themselves described it. A general description of the evolution of typical business disputes will then be given, before providing a more detailed analysis of the diverse types of business relationships observed and the role played by law in each of them.

In the rest of this book, excerpts from the interviews, translated from French, will serve to illustrate diverse points made by the interviewees in the study. In order to protect the anonymity of the interviewees and the confidentiality of the interviews, each interviewee is identified by a pseudonym. More information on the composition of the sample and the firms represented by each interviewee is provided in Appendix A.

The Business Communities of Dakar

Dakar is located on the Cap-Vert Peninsula on the Atlantic coast and is Africa's westernmost city. It is also one of the most important cities of West Africa, with a population amounting to over 2 million people, about one fourth of the country's total population. For a SME operating in sub-Saharan Africa, Dakar is a location with numerous advantages, of which the most important one is the political stability of Senegal, which has long been hailed as a symbol of democracy in a notoriously troubled region. The city nevertheless attained its current dominant economic and political position in West Africa only recently. The political troubles that shook the previously stable country of Côte d'Ivoire in the 2000s contributed to Dakar's rise to economic prominence, with many firms and organizations previously based in Abidjan relocating to Dakar in order to find political stability. But Dakar's new status as the economic capital of Francophone West Africa also has it downsides, the most important being an explosion of real estate prices in the area.

In order to understand the situation of the current business community of Dakar, it is fundamental to consider the history of the city. Europeans willing to develop trade in the region were initially attracted by the island of Gorée, a few miles from the coast, rather than the Cap-Vert Peninsula itself. By the middle of the sixteenth century, the island had become a base for the export of slaves by the Portuguese. After changing hands several times, Gorée fell to the French in 1677, while the mainland of Cap-Vert was still under the control of the Jolof Empire. The small village of Dakar, directly across from Gorée, serviced the island with food and drinking water.

Gorée started losing its privileged position in French colonial Africa with the development of the peanut trade. The growing population of the island began moving to the continent, but it is Rufisque, rather than Dakar, that came to replace Gorée as a trade center. In 1857, the French turned Dakar into a military post. The large infrastructure expenditures made by French colonial authorities to build and improve the port facilities later allowed the city to displace Rufisque. With the completion of the railway line between the city and the capital of Saint-Louis in 1885, Dakar became the leading urban center of the colony, and an important base for the conquest of the western Sudan. In 1902, Dakar replaced Saint-Louis as the capital of the Afrique Occidentale Française (AOF). The completion of the Dakar-Bamako railroad line, in the first quarter of the twentieth century, contributed to the consolidation of Dakar's dominant position in the French African Empire.

Towards the end of the nineteenth century, Saint-Louis, Rufisque and Gorée were recognized as French communes, with Dakar splitting off from Gorée as a separate commune in 1887. Under the French colonial regime, the inhabitants of the "Four Communes" (the "originaires") benefitted from a special treatment from colonial authorities, as they were extended rights of French citizenship. The Four Communes had a particularly strong French presence, and their inhabitants were well connected to the French political and commercial establishment. Until the beginning of the twentieth century, the French colonial policy was favorable to the emergence of a commercial Senegalese bourgeoisie. Amin (1976) reports that, in 1900, almost 800 Senegalese traders were registered with colonial authorities. Colonial policy changed between 1900 and 1920, as pacification and the establishment of French rule over new territories allowed the French trading posts to open inland offices and to compete with local traders. Under attack and with little access to direct import and credit, many Senegalese became employees of the colonial firms. The role of intermediaries between the French companies and the local population previously fulfilled by the local business class was taken on by newly arrived Lebanese immigrants. According to Marfaing and Sow (1999, 82–3), in 1935–36, Senegalese traders represented half of the licensed traders of Dakar, but only 15 percent of those operating in the countryside.

At independence, French and Lebanese firms largely dominated the Senegalese economy. Like most developing countries at this time, the country adopted a development policy based on import-substitution industrialization and heavy government involvement in economic activity. Some French firms were nationalized, and many state enterprises were created. The control of manufacturing enterprises passed to Senegalese businessmen with political connections to President Senghor's Parti Socialiste. A new "bureaucratic" bourgeoisie emerged, to the detriment of the established business class, whose presence was essentially limited to industries with low barriers to entry (trade, construction, and transportation). In parallel, the 1970s and 1980s saw the rise of a new category of Senegalese entrepreneurs in the commercial sector. Senegalese peasants operating in the declining peanut sector sought to evade the official peanut marketing board, leading to the expansion of contraband trading networks and the rise of new, powerful business groups. Many members of the Murid Islamic order, in particular, managed to accumulate large fortunes by trading in contraband goods. They also provided financial support to large numbers of young Senegalese trying to make a living in the city by reselling fraudulently imported goods in urban markets. Escaping the payment of taxes, fees, and social security charges, these new entrepreneurs became more competitive than their mostly French and Lebanese counterparts, who gradually withdrew from the import and distribution trade as well as many segments of light industry. This process, known as the "informalization" of Senegalese commerce, provided not only jobs to rural immigrants, but also cheap consumer goods that made it easier to cope with inflation, two factors that may account for the few governmental efforts made to fight contraband networks at the time.

From the mid-1980s, a series of market-oriented reforms took place under the aegis of the IMF and the World Bank. Trade was liberalized as a New Industrial Policy ("Nouvelle Politique Industrielle") provided for the suppression of quotas and licenses to import as well as the lowering of tariffs. In 1994, the regional currency (franc CFA), which was until then on a par with the French currency, was devalued by 50 percent as a way to increase levels of export and reduce budget deficits. The prices of imported goods increased dramatically, leading to a decrease of the spending power among the local population as well as increased poverty, contraband activity, and social unrest, with Dakar becoming the site of a series of violent demonstrations. Small- and medium-sized enterprises, in particular, had a difficult time facing the increase in the price of imports and the contraction of local demand for their goods. The combination of an increased recourse to consumer credit and the imposition of more stringent terms of payment from suppliers led to increased need for liquidities and higher levels of debt in this fraction of the business community. In the aftermath of the devaluation, a number of state-owned industries and public utilities were privatized, often to the benefit of French firms (France Télécom, Bouygues (water), Dagris (cotton), Advens (peanuts) etc.). Businessmen formerly privileged by their connections to the state saw their position compromised. In parallel, the Senegalese government was subjected to increasing pressure to widen the tax base by subjecting to taxation the numerous businesses operating under the radar of fiscal authorities

Despite deregulation and the rise of a new class of Senegalese businesspeople, the business community of Dakar remains highly stratified. Senegalese businessmen are still heavily concentrated in trade and some areas of light industry, while foreign, mostly French, capital is predominant in the manufacturing sector. It is estimated that over 250 French firms are in operation in Senegal, half of them as subsidiaries of France-based companies. Those firms often play a dominant role in many spheres of activity such as energy (SAR), telecommunications

(Sonatel), construction (Spie, Jean Lefebvre, Razel, Fougerolles), transportation (Bolloré, Air France), tourism (Sofitel, Senegal Tours, Club Med etc.), the food industry (Grands Moulins de Dakar, Compagnie Sucrière Sénégalaise, SOBOA, SOCAS), cement production (Sococim), and banking (Crédit Lyonnais, BNP, SGBS, CBAO). As to smaller firms, the lack of complete and recent statistics on Dakar's enterprises makes it difficult to properly assess their situation. Although small- and medium-sized firms are often said to represent about 90 percent of all firms operating in Senegal, this number comprises an unknown, but most probably very significant, number of micro-enterprises generally composed of a single individual of Senegalese origins and operating almost exclusively as petty traders or craftsmen. The notion of SMEs is generally defined so as to exclude those micro-enterprises and designate a large spectrum of firms counting between 5 and 250 employees. Senegalese SMEs exhibit a wide variety, both in terms of the ethnic origins of their members and the industry in which they operate.

The Senegalese economy is commonly described as comprising two distinct types of businesses, i.e. modern enterprises and firms operating in the informal sector. Due to the lack of consensus on the meaning of informality, it is hard to determine whether specific firms are in fact formal or informal. One common definition of informality refers to the extent to which a firm complies with applicable law, the most currently used indicator of informality being the failure to register with tax, employment or business licensing authorities. But it is also widely acknowledged that informality is more probably a matter of degree, with every firm complying with at least some formal rules and ignoring others. Compliance with the law may also be seen as only an indicator, rather than constitutive, of formality, understood more broadly as the fact, for a firm, to resort to modes of production and organization that sets it apart from registered or unregistered self-employed individuals. From this perspective, the transition from the informal to the formal is not so much a matter of compliance but of transforming daily strategies of survival into sustainable business activities.

In the Senegalese context, the problem of categorizing firms as formal or informal is amplified by the widespread use of the term "secteur informel" to designate the firms belonging to the trading networks that developed in the 1970s around the leaders of the Murid order. The "sector" thus comprises a majority of street or market vendors – also called Baol Baol, from the ancient name of the region of Diourbel, which hosts the holy Murid city of Touba – most often operating without a license as well as a significant number of larger, more or less formalized businesses originating from the same networks. In 1990, these firms created their own association, UNACOIS ("Union des commerçants et industriels du Sénégal"). Although controlled by the wealthy traders who dominate the trade sector, UNACOIS clearly positions itself as the defender of small businesses and "national" interests against the "foreign capital" dominating the "modern" sector. UNACOIS has also taken a position against the arrival in Dakar of immigrant Chinese importers, selling directly to consumers and Dakar's petty traders, qualifying their presence as "unfair competition".

Business Law in Senegal

French law was first imported to Senegal during the colonial period, with legislation being introduced in the colony on a piecemeal basis and with adaptations deemed to be required by local circumstances. The imported laws included the Civil Code and the Commercial Code. As in the rest of West Africa, a dual legal regime was put in place: while colonial law governed French citizens, customary law remained applicable to relationships between non-citizens (Rolland and Lampué 1931). At independence, the existing laws remained in force and were nationalized. As part of the efforts to "modernize" the country, almost all the branches of the law were reformed, in line with the French model (David and Jauffret-Spinosi 1988, 658). A new Code of Obligations was adopted, on which the influence of customary law proved negligible (Salacuse 1969, 232).

The idea of harmonizing the commercial laws of the different countries of Francophone Africa surfaced immediately after independence. The need for a harmonized legal framework was recognized in 1961 in the "Convention de coopération en matière de justice" signed by the members of the "Union africaine et malgache", who then committed to harmonize their commercial laws. In 1962, Kéba M'Baye, then a member of the Senegalese Ministry of Justice, proposed to the Union the creation of the "Bureau Africain et Malgache de Recherche et d'Études Législatives"[1] (BAMREL), whose mission was to elaborate uniform laws directly applicable in the member states. After a few years, though, BAMREL ceased to function due to a lack of funds and the idea of a general harmonization of business law was laid aside.

The harmonization project resurfaced in the 1990s, when it was debated in several different summits. In April 1991, in Ouagadougou, the Ministers of Finance of the countries of the *zone franc* decided to organize a reflection on the feasibility of a project to harmonize business law, with a view to rationalizing the legal environment in which firms conducted their activities (Issa-Sayegh and Lohoues-Oble 2002, 95). Six months later, in Paris, a team of experts (called *mission de haut niveau*) was formed and put in charge of assessing the political and technical feasibility of the project. The team, which comprised seven members,

---

1   African and Malagasy Legal Research Office.

was led by Kéba M'Baye, then Judge of the International Court of Justice and former President of the Senegal's Supreme Court and Conseil Constitutionnel. On September 17, 1992, the mission filed its final report. A three-member steering committee (*directoire*) was formed and given responsibility for drafting an international treaty and identifying the areas of the law to be harmonized. The draft treaty establishing the "Organization pour l'harmonisation en Afrique du droit des affaires" (OHADA) was signed by 14 countries[2] on 17 October 1993, in Port-Louis (Mauritius), and entered into force about a year later.

Although the Organization is open to all African Union members and other states upon invitation, the vast majority of its 16 present members are Francophone and former French colonies or mandate territories of Africa.[3] All but Guinea and Comores are also members of the Franc monetary zone.

The Rationale for OHADA

In conformity with the new development approach, the objective of the OHADA reform is to attract foreign investors, facilitate trade, and favor the emergence of a dynamic private sector. As stated in the Preamble of the Treaty creating the Organization, OHADA is meant to create a new development cluster in Africa by establishing a "climate of trust" through the implementation of a "harmonized, simple, modern and adapted" business law applied "with diligence" in order to "guarantee the legal security of economic activities in order to promote their growth and foster investment" (OHADA 1997). As mentioned in Article 1 of the Treaty, the reform process has three major aspects: the "modernization" of the law, its "harmonization" within the OHADA region, and the creation of appropriate procedures, including arbitration, for the settlement of contractual disputes.

Observers have noted that OHADA's name does not reflect its true mission, which is not legal harmonization but the implementation of an "aggressively top-down" (Dickerson 2005, 59) scheme for the uniformization of business laws. The "harmonization" sought by OHADA consists in the "de-nationalization" of the law-making and judicial processes, by replacing national political and judicial institutions with new regional instances in charge of adopting and applying the new law. For this purpose, the OHADA Treaty provides for the creation of four supranational institutions. The Council of Ministers, which is comprised

---

2   Benin, Burkina Faso, Cameroon, the Central African Republic, Chad, the Comoros, Congo, Côte d'Ivoire, Gabon, Equatorial Guinea, Mali, Niger, Senegal, and Togo.

3   The exceptions are Guinea-Bissau (Portuguese), Equatorial Guinea (Spanish), and the English-speaking provinces of Cameroon (which was a French/British mandate territory).

of the Ministers of Justice and Ministers responsible for Finance of the member countries, is at the apex of the OHADA system. It elects or appoints the members of the other institutions, approves the annual harmonization program prepared by the Permanent Secretary Office and, in consultation with the Common Court of Justice and Arbitration (CCJA), adopts the legislation prepared by the Secretary. The last institution is the Regional School of the Judiciary ("École régionale de la Magistrature" or ERSUMA), which provides training for the judges and judiciary staff of the member States.

Legal integration presents two major advantages over national legal reform. First, the pooling of national resources allows the Member States to create a better legal and judicial system than they would have built on their own (Kirsch 1998, 131). A single body of law published by a single organization in an official journal greatly simplifies the dissemination process, and allows for the creation of more important markets for legal textbooks and legal education programs. Legal and judicial professionals also become able to exchange ideas and experiences, leading to the emergence of a legal profession better equipped to work at the international level (Forneris 2001, 5). The OHADA reform thus represents a useful tool to shake up the quasi-monopoly of Western legal firms in the regional legal market. The regionalization of reform efforts also contributes to making the new laws more attractive: by providing an integrated legal framework, the OHADA initiative aims at facilitating the work of firms interested in operating at a regional rather than national level, thus making the whole region more attractive to foreign investors.

At the normative level, harmonization is effected through the adoption of Uniform Acts. The Permanent Secretary is in charge of preparing the new legislation, in consultation with the governments of the member states. One or many experts are first commissioned to prepare a draft act, which is then submitted for review and comment to each national government, generally acting through a "national committee". The adoption of the final version of the Act is then made by the Council of Ministers and requires the unanimous approval of the representatives of the member states present and voting. Two thirds of the member states must be represented in the voting process. After its adoption, an Act becomes directly applicable in each member state, notwithstanding any conflict with previous or subsequent enactment of municipal laws. No implementing legislation is required.

The scope of the OHADA reform extends well beyond commercial law *per se* to cover the entire legal framework applying to economic activities. Article 2 of the Treaty mentions as coming within the ambit of the Organization such matters as company law, the legal status of commercial operators, the recovery of debts, securities, enforcement measures, insolvency proceedings, arbitration, employment, accounting law, sales, transport, as well as any other subject which the Council of Ministers may decide to include as falling within the definition of business law. Eight Uniform Acts have been adopted so far, with respect to general commercial law (April 1997), company law (April 1997), collateral law (April 1997), debt recovery procedures and measures of execution (April 1998), bankruptcy (April 1998), arbitration (March 1999), accounting (February 2000) and transportation of goods by land (March 2003) and cooperatives (December 2010). Draft Uniform Acts on contract law, telecommunications, consumer protection and employment law have been prepared but not adopted.

At the judicial level, the main unification institution is the Common Court of Justice and Arbitration (CCJA). It consists of seven judges elected for seven years and chosen among the nationals of the member states. The CCJA has jurisdiction over all matters pertaining to the application of OHADA law. It can hear appeals of the decisions pronounced by the appellate courts of the member states (save decisions regarding penal sanctions pronounced by these courts) and has jurisdiction in cassation with respect to the decisions not subject to ordinary appeal. As a result of the CCJA jurisdiction, the national courts retain jurisdiction with respect to OHADA law only in first instance and on ordinary appeal. Where a case reaches the highest appellate level, the national Supreme Court concerned must decline jurisdiction over the case and send the matter to the CCJA. The decisions of the CCJA are final and enforceable in conformity with the rules of civil procedure applicable to national judgments in the state in which enforcement is sought. The CCJA also serves as an arbitration center; it can name and confirm arbitrators, monitors the progress of the arbitration proceedings, and examine arbitration awards before they are signed.

The decision to locate the CCJA in Abidjan has been the subject of some debate in the OHADA community. Local lawyers have argued that the additional costs associated with the need to travel to a distant location might prevent litigants from appealing to the court. In addition, although any lawyer entitled to appear before the courts of the member states can appear before the CCJA, the fact that lawyers who do not reside in Abidjan must elect domicile there for the duration of the proceedings might give Ivoirian lawyers an unfair advantage over their colleagues from other countries. Reporting on the meeting held by the Senegalese Bar concerning OHADA, N'Doye concluded on a critical note, stating that the goal of African integration should not take precedence over people's legal security of the people and take the bread out of lawyers' mouths (N'Doye 1995, 8). The CCJA statistics suggest that these concerns are not without foundation: more than half of the 918 appeals initiated since 1990 come from Côte d'Ivoire (Dalmeida Mele 2010, 59). It must be noted, however, that the number of decisions rendered by the CCJA is fairly small, with about 500 to 600 judgments delivered since 1990 (Beauchard and Koko 2011, 19).

An African Reform?

The proponents of the OHADA initiative are prone to insist on its "Africanness". And yet, one cannot fail to notice the important and even determinant role that non-Africans played in the design and implementation of the reform. The *Coopération française* played a central role in the launch and promotion of the project, and France provided financial and technical assistance and financed most of the capital appreciation fund. Other funders include the European Union, the United Nations Program for Development, and to a lesser extent Japan, Belgium and the African Development Bank. More recently, the World Bank also joined the common effort and started to provide financial and technical support. As to the harmonized laws, they were mostly drafted by European experts, including the Paris offices of a number of US law firms (Ofosu-Amaah 2000, 45). French law, as it existed when the Acts were drafted, is the most important source of inspiration for the Acts, the second being the law of Guinea, whose *Code des activités économiques* was partly copied in the Uniform Act on company law (Paillusseau 2004) .

France's deep involvement in and influence on the reform process, which involved only limited national input, bring to light the issues of the political legitimacy of the Acts and their level of adaptation to local conditions. Although the reform process involved the creation of "national committees" in which local professionals could participate, they were not always properly constituted or operative (Ofosu-Amaah 2000,45). In 2011, a meeting of representatives of the national committees came to the conclusion that the committees still lacked the levels of visibility and local presence required to properly support state institutions and business communities (*Commissions nationales*, OHADA 2011, 7). In consequence, and although the actual contribution of the national committees to the design of the reforms of the 1990s remains unclear, they seem unlikely to have had a strong impact on the content of the new laws or popular buy-in of the reform.

The relatively contained controversy about the African character of OHADA eventually gave way to a much-publicized debate about the choice of French law as a basis for reform. The debate was sparked by the publication, and endorsement by the World Bank, of a series of studies conducted by a group of American economists led by Rafael La Porta, and later known as the LLSV group, from the names of its most active members. Based on an investigation of the impact of the "origin" of legal systems on the quality of investment climates, the LLSV studies concluded that, regulation being heavier and less protective of property rights in civil law systems, such systems are less efficient and attractive than systems based on the common law. The inclusion of these findings in the "Doing Business" report for 2004 generated a large amount of negative reaction in the French legal community. At the beginning of 2007, the publication of a newsletter by UNIDA,[4] the Paris-based organization set up to promote the OHADA process, sparked a vocal debate with the World Bank by qualifying the Doing Business methodology as "questionable" (UNIDA 2007a). The debate escalated in the following weeks, with UNIDA qualifying the whole Doing Business exercise as "random" and "dangerous", before calling all states to confront the president of the Bank with respect to this "purely ideological and extremely dangerous and destabilizing" exercise likened to a game of "sorcerer's apprentice" (UNIDA 2007b). Things eventually settled between the Bank and the proponents of OHADA, with the Bank starting to provide financial and technical assistance to the project, including injecting 1.5 million dollars to "reinforce" the national committees and supporting the modernization of national registry systems.

In 2008, a project to revise and redraft the Uniform Acts was initiated. The Bank's Investment Climate Facility for Africa has been instrumental in this process, including the review of the strengths and weaknesses of the OHADA legislation and the preparation of new versions of two Uniform Acts that were adopted in December 2010. The Act on general commercial law made a new status of *entreprenant* available to individual enterprises whose total revenues do not exceed a certain threshold. *Entreprenants* are exempted from having to enroll at the *Registre du Commerce et du Crédit Mobilier* and can operate by virtue of a simple declaration made to the local court's registry. The new Act on secured transactions was also modified to incorporate in OHADA law the changes made to French law in the 2000s. The reform process is still ongoing with respect to the other Acts.

Although there is an important and growing body of literature on OHADA, it mostly consists in analyses of the new laws and their implementation by national courts and the CCJA. Very little is known on the impact of the reform on its end-users, i.e. the firms operating in the OHADA region, with the few studies conducted on this matter focusing mostly on legal professionals, French firms or local large firms. The lack of judicial statistics at the level of national courts also makes any assertion concerning the effect of the OHADA reform on litigation impossible to verify.

More information is available with respect to the promotion of arbitration. The OHADA project put a strong emphasis on the creation of arbitration mechanisms, and the adoption of the Uniform Act on arbitration inaugurated the CCJA as a regional arbitration center. However, the CCJA's role in this respect remains underdeveloped, with only 37 cases submitted between 1990 and 2010 (Ledongo

---

4   "Association pour l'Unification du droit en Afrique" (Association for the unification of law in Africa).

2010). In parallel with the implementation of the OHADA reform, the end of the 1990s saw the introduction of arbitration in Senegalese law. In 1998, the Dakar Chamber of Commerce created an arbitration center. Conceived as a way to palliate the insufficiencies of the judicial system (Alibert 1999, 1037), the center combines arbitration and mediation functions. In 2009, a local business magazine quoted Mamadou Lamine Niang, then president of the CCIAD, as evaluating at 50 the number of sentences rendered by the Centre since its foundation (Réussir 2009); this amounts to less than 10 cases a year.

The Business Climate

As any visitor to the city could not fail to notice, firms operating in Dakar have to deal with a number of factors and constraints rarely faced by their counterparts based in industrialized economies, and over which they have no or very little control. Local climatic conditions are one of them. The rainy season that extends from June to October (*l'hivernage*) is a constant source of problems, as access to certain regions of the country or neighborhoods of the city become difficult or impossible, forcing firms to take exceptional measures to prevent supply shortages. The country is also affected by periodic droughts. With agriculture being a major source of revenue in rural areas, drought and other factors affecting agricultural production have a direct impact on demand for certain kinds of goods as well as the capacity of clients in rural areas to settle past debts.

The impact of the *hivernage* on transportation is amplified by the inadequacy of the transportation infrastructures servicing the region. Partly because it has grown rapidly in the last years, Dakar suffers from important traffic congestion problems that the simultaneous construction of a number of new roads and highways aims at solving. In the meantime, important road works have made access to the town's business center as well as transportation from one neighborhood to another very difficult for many years. Unpredictable variations in the time required to go from one place to another represent significant obstacles to making plans and holding appointments.

Another source of concern is the notorious unreliability of the state-owned electricity supplier, SENELEC. Daily, unannounced power cuts have affected the whole country, including Dakar's business and industrial districts, for many years. A recovery plan was adopted in 2011 that provides for the temporary exploitation of two power stations by American private company APR Energy in order to allow SENELEC, which is on the verge of bankruptcy, to focus on the maintenance and renovation of its other stations. For businesses, the frequency of the cuts means they have to invest in alternative sources of supply to avoid the interruption to their operations. This is particularly problematic for small firms in the manufacturing sector, which often cannot afford the generators required to operate their equipment. Babacar, who heads a firm in the garment industry, mentioned that power cuts could significantly delay production: "if we deliver a week later than planned, the client, even if he is in Senegal and knows about the cuts, might still blame us for not having our own generator."

Even though Senegal has traditionally been the most politically stable country of the region, it is not immune from political troubles, as the events that surrounded the 2012 Presidential elections show. The political instability affecting the African continent also impacts on the country. The eruption of a "civil war" in Côte d'Ivoire, which until the end of the 1990s was considered among the best investment locations in West Africa, only reinforced the impression that stability must never be taken for granted in Africa. Political problems at the regional level not only affect firms doing business across borders but also impact on their business partners. More generally, the reputation of Africa as an unstable continent is seen as a contributing factor to what many African firms perceive as the reluctance of foreign firms to take risks or even enter into business relationships with African firms. As Lamine puts it, "it is not about the people; it's that things can go off any time. I know people who were doing business in Abidjan, they never got paid: how can you get paid by someone who is stuck in the middle of a civil war?"

Those problems are often compounded by the precarious financial situation of a large proportion of firms and individuals. Widespread poverty means that many final users of basic goods are vulnerable to even relatively small shocks; for the firms that supply those goods, that means that they need to deal with variations in demand and payment problems. For most firms, the absence of the financial cushion needed to face such contingencies forces them to deal with late payment from their clients by passing the problem to their own suppliers. Performance problems thus tend to ripple through the whole economic chain, forming a vicious circle of non-compliance.

Financial constraints are not restricted to small- and medium-sized firms. Recent history has also demonstrated that "structurally adjusted" state institutions and large local firms (many of whom were previously owned or supported by the state) are no longer immune from financial problems. For example, the future of the Industries Chimiques du Sénégal (ICS), one of the largest companies in operation in Senegal, was the subject of much speculation at the time of fieldwork. Then on the verge of bankruptcy, the company was eventually "saved" in 2007 by new injection of money by its shareholders, including the Senegalese government. Although no interviewee counted the ICS as a direct client, many expressed concern about the possible consequence of the loss of thousands of well-paid jobs on Dakar's and Senegal's economies as well as on their own firm's operations. As one interviewee said, "ICS represents 2,000 jobs, and they threaten to eliminate all of them; for a country counting 10 millions of people, 2,000 jobs are a lot. Among those 2,000 employees, I must have at least 10 good, safe clients. When they close the company, I will lose them" (Babacar).

Among all the economic actors that fail to pay their bills in a timely manner, state institutions are considered the worst of all. A majority of interviewees mentioned that the state's propensity to delay payments to its suppliers, sometimes for many months or even years, constituted a major problem. Even firms that used to seek doing business with state institutions may now be reluctant to submit bids for tender. According to Alassane,

> You need to be strong to work with the state. We're in the process of figuring to what extent we want to get involved in state projects, because, you know, the problem i … cash flows are the sinews of war. You may have clients that will pay for sure, but if it takes you a year to get the mone …

Robert, who works in the construction industry, was still waiting for bills to be paid four years after the end of the contract. Moustapha, head of a firm that offers management-training services, noted that "there is a big difference between dealing with the state and dealing with the private sector. Private firms take a week to pay at most, compared to three months with the stat …" The payment delays from state institutions were attributed to diverse factors, including a tight financial situation and bureaucratic constraints, with "money passing through 100 different offices" before getting to the right pockets.

Due to local sources of uncertainty and financial constraints, Dakar's business environment is characterized by a high incidence of contractual breaches. Almost all the firms met acknowledged that contractual violations are frequent, and many identified them as one of the most important issues they have to deal with as managers. Dealing with financial difficulties and their impact on production is an important aspect of their daily work and the most pressing issue they have to face. Lack of contractual discipline forces managers to constantly juggle their various commitments in order to find the liquidities they need. Having insufficient working capital may make firms unable to acquire the goods they need in a timely manner, thus slowing down production.

Many financial problems are ultimately tied to the lack of access to short-term and long-term financing in the form of bank loans, bank overdrafts, or supplier credit. Banks are often blamed for what is perceived as their unwillingness to support Senegalese SMEs. For Aicha, e.g. the banks operating in Dakar "are very cautious, they do not trust SMEs at all. They won't take any risk with a SME." Reports on the Senegalese financial sector confirm that such perceptions are not without foundation. A study conducted in 2010 concluded that Senegalese SMEs have little access to bank financing, partly due to the absence of financial products adapted to their specific needs (République du Sénégal 2010, 8).

Courts: Beyond Access

West Africa is widely considered to be among the world's most corrupt places, and Senegal is no exception. According to Transparency International, which defines itself as a leader in the fight against corruption, Senegal ranks 112 out of 183 countries for perceived levels of public officials corruption, with a score of 2.9 out of 10 (Transparency International 2011). Surprisingly then, few firms mentioned corruption as a major issue. Those who did referred mostly to import/export matters or issues relating to the application of social security regulation. In general, interviewees were far more likely to blame state institutions for being unreliable than for being corrupt.

With respect to the judicial system, interviewees were generally confident in the quality of the judicial decisions rendered. Concerns about judicial corruption were expressed in only a few instances, mostly by interviewees from non-African origins. This is particularly striking when one considers that, in parallel, interviewees referred to a certain number of cases of corruption from State representatives or employees of other firms. Interestingly, corrupt practices were more often identified as having an impact not on the quality of judicial decisions *per se* but on the total duration of the judicial process, and were often blamed on legal officials or professionals rather than judges. As Jacques said, "if you manage to get your file through the whole process things will be all right, but some people will try to prevent it to get through. I think some files get stuck at some point, from time to time."

Although legal costs did not emerge as a significant problem in themselves, a few interviewees also took issue with the disproportion between the otherwise reasonable costs incurred in recovering a debt and the amounts involved in small-size transactions, which often form the bulk of their business. A related issue concerns the fact that many transactions made with unsophisticated business players (including many "informal" firms) are left undocumented, making them hard to prove in court.

A third of the interviewees mentioned having filed formal legal claims in relation to business disputes. A few more had been in contact with the judicial system in other circumstances, either as defendants or witnesses in business or other types of cases. In the case of six of the interviewees, their experience as claimants was limited to one or two cases. The other interviewees with experience with the civil courts could be described as repeat users, although the number of cases they file amounts to only a handful a year. Previous contact with the civil courts did not seem to have a major impact on interviewees' views of the judicial system, with no significant differences between the opinions of past users and those of interviewees without experience with the judicial system.

An overwhelming majority of interviewees said they would consider court use only as a very last resort and in exceptional cases only. At first sight, such an attitude seems to confirm the negative perceptions of the local judicial system that dominate in the legal literature. Yet, a closer look at the reasons accounting for the reluctance of interviewees to litigate their claims reveals that negative perceptions of the court system seem to have little impact on legal behaviour. Interviewees almost never cited legal costs, legal complexity, corruption, and judicial competence as a major consideration in their decisions. In general, they viewed the Senegalese legal and judicial systems in a rather positive light, with laws "allowing firms to function and develop" (Moustapha) and courts filled with "competent people who do their jobs right" (Almamy). Most of them thought that the court system worked reasonably well, and many said they would consider using it if they really needed to. As for the legal framework, the few complaints voiced essentially concerned the rigidity of Senegalese labor law.

This suggests that, in order to account for the unpopularity of the solutions provided by Dakar courts to the problems faced by Dakar SMEs, it is necessary to go beyond an examination of the functioning of the judicial system. Neither the frequency of contractual breach in Dakar nor the reactions of local economic actors to this reality can be properly understood without taking proper account of the local environment in which SMEs operate and the specific constraints they face. In this respect, one of the concerns most often voiced by interviewees concerned the sums one can actually expect to be able to collect at the end of the judicial process, especially when non-payment is the consequence of financial difficulties: a judicial decision does not provide debtors with money to pay. Waiting until the other party is actually able to pay his debt was often described as a better way to get at least part of one's money back. In addition, seizing one partner's assets was sometimes described as the best way to run him out of his business and thus lose a client.

Overall, however, the most important concern of firms relates to the time needed to obtain an enforceable decision. Remarks about the justice system being too slow figure in almost all accounts. In the absence of reliable court records, the time needed to obtain a judicial decision cannot be ascertained with precision. Informal conversations with lawyers in Dakar indicated that the delay needed to obtain a final judicial decision in Dakar compares with the situation that prevails in Canada, thus suggesting that the problem thus might not be with the time required to get a decision but with the impact that any delay is likely to have on litigants. For firms unable to deal with the absence of the supplies or sums of money they were counting on to pursue their activities, getting part of one's money or supplies rapidly is preferable to the possibility of being compensated at a later point, and litigation is used only where it is the only option but for "lumping" one's claim. Yet, even in cases of fraud or clear dishonesty, the efficiency of courts is limited, law being ultimately unable to deter "crooks" from trying to rip people off. The possibility of obtaining compensation in cases of fraud tends to be remote, since crooks tend to use false names and addresses, run away, or escape seizures by putting their assets under someone else's name. In consequence, prevention remains the preferred way to protect oneself against fraudulent practices.

Chapter 4

Doing Business in Dakar:
Contracts, Trust, and Relationships

Dakar SMEs see non-compliance as having negative consequences on their business and consider the resolution of contractual problems an important part of their job. They also see courts as not very useful for this purpose: judicial decisions do not make bad payers more able to pay, and do not provide firms with solutions to the pressing problems they face. Prevention is thus the best solution. Businesspeople are generally aware of the need to limit the risks they run by reducing the probability of contractual breach and/or the potential consequences of such breaches. For this purpose, they can either choose to engage only, or primarily, in transactions involving low levels of risk. According to game theorists, they can also choose to rely on informal contract enforcement mechanisms in order to deter their partners from breaching their contract In the present chapter, we will review the strategies used by Dakar SMEs to manage business risk as well as the downsides and limited efficiency of such strategies in the local context. We will then see how firms deal with the risks that they are unable to avoid, by looking at the various methods they use to prevent and solve contractual disputes.

Limiting Risks: Choosing the Right Partners

In theory, there are two main ways to limit contractual risks. One of them consists in refusing to enter into a contract unless the deal is a spot-market transaction with cash payment and full inspection of the goods. But this strategy, characteristic of what Fafchamps and Minten (2001) call "flea-market economies", is not well adapted to the conduct of more complex business activities. An alternative strategy involves engaging in risky transactions with reliable partners only. This solution is also of limited relevance in the Dakar context. On the one hand, the small size of the local market and firms' limited access to external markets in which they can get the supplies they need or sell their products severely limit the pool from which they can choose their suppliers. On the other hand, intense competition from both smaller and larger firms often forces SMEs to take more risks than they would like in order to "win the deal".

Selecting Suppliers

A major problem encountered by firms operating in Dakar concerns the limited size of the local supplier pool. The underdevelopment of the manufacturing sector means that local production is inexistent for an important number of goods. For a majority of firms operating in the trade and manufacturing sectors, this entails that an important part of their supplies have to be imported from Europe, Asia or North America, either directly or through locally based intermediaries. Dealing directly with foreign-based suppliers on a regular basis allows firms them to get better prices than if the same goods were acquired through an intermediary. However, since importing entails hassle and additional delay, it is an option only where delivery time is not an issue: "usually we import from Spain or Italy, it is cheaper; but when the delay is short, we have someone in Dakar who can deliver in 24 hours. But it is more expensive" (Thierno). For some, importing can also increase risks of contractual breach for two reasons. First, defective products cannot be returned easily and disputes about quality are hard to solve at a distance. Secondly, business from small African firms is not actively sought after by foreign firms, who tend to give priority to larger, more established partners. Alassane, who works in automotive sales, noted that orders from foreign exporters often arrive late: "if we order five containers from a French supplier that also has orders from China or Brazil for twenty containers, no matter how nice you are, how good is your relationship, the bigger deals will take precedence. It's normal business."

For many firms, building business relationships with foreign firms remains a challenge. One issue concerns the reluctance of foreign exporters to grant credit and their insistence on using costly financial instruments such as letters of credit to secure payment and limit their own risks. What is seen as the reluctance of foreign businesses to deal with local firms is often attributed to the general reputation of African firms as unreliable, or the African continent as too risky a place for business, which leads to a significant deficit of trust in Senegalese firms: "Europeans trust you [North Americans] but they do not trust us [Africans]. Even in China or Japan, they ask for irrevocable letters of credit, confirmed by a bank! What does it mean? That's what you ask from thieves and murderers!"(Saliou).

As for local suppliers, their number is often quite limited where certain types of goods are concerned or large quantities are needed, with markets often being oligopolistic. Firms seeking to place large orders generally have to buy from one of the very few large firms in a position to fill them. Thierno, head of a medium-sized firm in the manufacturing sector, always buys from the largest firms in the market, "because they can meet our needs: they have large inventories and they can even have additional stock shipped by plane if need be." It is also difficult to locate reliable local suppliers for products of higher quality. Firms in need of such goods often have to pay the higher prices charged by well-established firms until they can locate alternative suppliers offering products of equivalent quality (including in terms of after-sales service).

Even in the segments in which many firms compete for the same clients, variations in the composition of their inventories mean that a specific product is rarely available at more than one place at the same time. As Jacques mentions, "it is hard for us to maintain an appropriate inventory, so clients just go for the supplier who has the product in stock". Clients are thus forced to shop around to find the supplier who can fulfill their needs, relegating price considerations to the background. In cases where a certain good is in fact available from many different sources, price is the determining factor in the buying decision. However, the precarious financial situation of firms means that, although they want to obtain the best price they can, they also pay particular attention to the financial conditions imposed by suppliers. The establishment of long-term business relationships with a supplier is often seen as key to obtaining credit: "at first, suppliers don't trust you; it takes time and effort to convince them to sell on credit" (Babacar).

Long-term relationships also allow firms to achieve other economic efficiencies, such as economizing on search and negotiation costs. This is not negligible in cases where the supplier pool consists of a plethora of small firms offering products or services of varying prices and quality. It may also be particularly valuable in places like Dakar, where business dealings start with a round of negotiations: "that's the major interest of having a regular supplier: he knows how much we are ready to pay, we don't have to negotiate as much each time; prices get more stable" (Pierre). But, even where such long-term relationships are established, they are rarely exclusive and do not prevent firms from shopping around for new partners and better prices, and renegotiating contractual terms: "having a relationship with or sympathy for someone does not allow this person to charge me prices that are not correct – I know what prices I can get on the market" (Almamy).

Screening Clients

The main risk associated with dealing with clients is the risk of non- or late payment. Only one firm, involving the sale of second-hand clothes to low-income clients, dealt with this risk by entering into spot market transactions alone. Less drastic solutions include refusing to extend credit to certain categories of clients considered too risky, for example state institutions, which are in the unique position of being able to impose their conditions on private firms while being notoriously slow payers. Friends and family members are also considered to be bad payers, as they often feel entitled to borrow money or obtain goods on credit with no stringent obligation to repay. In consequence, "dealing with relatives always gets you into trouble" (Aliou) and should be avoided.

Avoiding certain kinds of clients has an important drawback – it may prevent firms from attracting enough customers to stay in business. In view of the importance of credit in the life of firms and individuals alike, refusing to extend credit may turn away clients whose business might nonetheless be profitable in the long run. Many of the firms met seemed somewhat torn between their need to keep their customers and attract new ones, and the need to stay afloat financially to ensure their survival. A strategy used by many interviewees to increase their competitiveness without increasing their financial risks consists in differentiating one's products from competing offers, for example by emphasizing their superior quality and/or exclusive character or other features such as the provision of after-sale services. This also seemed to be the preferred way to deal with the "unfair" competition of firms operating (totally or partially) informally, which operate at lower costs than formal SMEs. Alternative strategies to attract clients included resorting to networks of relationships or giving "gifts" to establish contact with potential clients and influence them in one's favor. Most of the time, however, SMEs trying to break into or survive in competitive markets have to match or beat the prices and other financial conditions offered by existing firms. Abdou, who heads a firm in the trade sector, mentions that "when we opened, there were only two of us on this market. We almost never sold on credit back then. Now everybody does what we do, if we don't sell on credit we just won't sell at all".

Price and credit facilities often work in combination when devising the "best offer" to make. For example, one interviewee, a retailer selling exclusive, higher-end clothing items, managed to attract customers toward his more expensive products by having the price of the goods sold deducted each month from their pay check by their employer. But agreeing to extend credit in order to attract a client may create a dangerous precedent when the client's reliability over the long term cannot be ascertained. Aliou indicated that he sometimes solved such dilemmas by offering lower, "end of season" cash prices to clients he wants to attract, and then switching to credit sales at higher prices as the relationship develops.

What emerges from the interviews is that market position, rather than the need to reduce risk levels, may be the most important determinant of business decisions relating to the selection of partners and the determination of contractual terms. Where competition comes from firms with financial resources that enable them to offer hard-to-match credit facilities, SMEs often have to take greater risks than they would like in order to win the deal. As Almamy notes, "as we are new on the market, and smaller than our competitors, they have financial resources that we don't have, they can advance money to their clients. So the clients have more bargaining power when they come to us." The capacity of clients to meet their obligations also often correlates with their market power. Low-risk, reliable clients are few and generally have the capacity to strike better deals and impose stringent financial conditions that make life difficult for less powerful market players. In comparison, clients in less advantageous markets positions may be easier to get and agree to pay higher prices, but are more vulnerable to contingencies and less likely to pay on time when credit is extended.

Local social norms also emerge as having a certain impact on firms' credit-granting practices. In Dakar, it is widely believed that one has to lend money to relatives and friends, including by "selling" on credit. This obligation to sell on credit, irrespective of the buyer's capacity to repay, can also extend beyond one's own circle to encompass persons introduced by others. For some, this constraint, although it may constitute an important obstacle to business profitability, is simply impossible to evade:

> in Senegal, there is this custom that, when someone is recommended to you, you can't say no. That's the way things are here, we have this custom. So sometimes we have to let someone leave with a product, even though we think this person will never pay for it; we just have to (Abdou).

Limiting the impact of this custom may require some imagination. Cheik describes his personal tactics in the following terms:

> For my part, I don't lend money, I give money. For example, if someone comes to me and asks for, let's say, 100,000 francs, I won't lend him 100,000. I will lend him 20,000 – 20,000 is nothing for me; so I lend him 20,000, and I am sure I will never see this person again. He will do everything he can to avoid me: that's it – I got rid of him!

Keeping a balance between short-term imperatives (i.e. cash flow management) and longer-term goals (i.e. increasing revenues) tends to be a challenge for all SMEs. But, whereas start-up and very small firms see attracting new clients as fundamental, "larger" and better-established enterprises tend to be more sensitive to financial management issues and more likely to "rationalize" their credit and debt collection functions by creating specialized departments and procedures. Having dealt with financial problems in the past also seems to lead managers to adopt more conservative credit-granting practices. As Cheik indicates:

> I faced important problems because of my clients; because for my part I pay cash, I do not have liquidities. So I had to harden my commercial policies: I

don't sell on credit anymore, or when I do I ask for a bank draft. I realized that's the way suppliers manage to survive here.

Risk Management and "Trust"

The environment in which Dakar SMEs operates severely limits the efficiency of "screening" and "spot transaction" methods for preventing contractual breach. Rather than avoiding risk, firms have to devise ways to deal with it as well as they can. A major challenge for SMEs consists in correctly assessing beforehand the level of risk associated with potential transactions in order to determine whether it is worth taking or not. The risks attached to a particular transaction depend on two distinct factors: the probability that the agreement will be breached, and the consequences attached to the breach in question. The potential impact of a breach may be lessened through diverse means, such as dealing with more than one supplier, fixing limits to the amount of credit that can be granted to a single client or asking for a down payment covering one's costs before completing an order. In addition to these strategies, the firms met often attempted to reduce contractual risk by fixing the amount at risk in a transaction in function of the "trustworthiness" of the partner involved, with transactions representing a significant level of risk being reserved for people they "trust".

Being considered trustworthy is a complicated matter in Dakar. Because of the uncertain environment in which they operate, Dakar economic actors tend to see perfect contractual compliance as rarely achievable. Trust therefore has less to do with the probability that someone will fulfill his contractual duties as planned than with his willingness to do his best to minimize the impact of a potential breach on his partner as much as possible in light of the circumstances. Trustworthiness comprises two elements: the (primarily financial) capacity to satisfy one's obligations, and one's willingness to do so. Assessing trustworthiness thus first requires distinguishing *bona fide* firms from crooks looking for an opportunity to take one's money and run. It is often a matter of experience: "after a while, you know who you deal with, who is serious, rigorous in what he says and does. So that's pretty simple" (Aicha). Such impressions can be supplemented by paying a visit to the shop or office of prospective partners or information gleaned from diverse sources. In the absence of formal credit rating or other reliable information mechanisms, business and social networks represent the most important repository of (more or less) reliable information on business reputation, and are routinely used to identify and get in touch with potential partners.

Despite the size of Dakar and its status within the West African region, interviewees often mentioned that the town is still small enough for people to get to know almost all the major players in their line of business. In addition, the various networks of relationships that exist in the city often overlap and create numerous types of links between apparently unrelated actors. In Dakar, everyone knows everyone else, and information flows easily from one circle to another. Friends, relatives, colleagues, or business relations can be put to use to gather specific information on a firm's situation. As Alassane reports:

> if someone wants to open an account with us, we ask for banking information; but the bank is not obliged to give us this information. So we resort to informal circuits: we always find someone at the bank that we know and who can provide us with the information we need.

Interestingly, information about past contractual violations does not seem particularly sought after or considered when making decisions. This is because past conduct toward other people is seen as constituting a reliable indicator of future conduct only where it clearly reveals a serious lack of ethics or a state of impending bankruptcy. Otherwise, direct business dealings remain the best way to assess the trustworthiness of a particular partner. Trust then builds incrementally as parties get to know each other and agree to gradually increase the level of risk they are ready to take. Finally, the permanent severing of business relationships with partners in breach was rarely cited as an appropriate way to limit contractual risk. In view of the few options available to firms when time comes to select business partners, refusing to deal with someone on the basis of past contractual breach alone is a luxury that many of them cannot afford: "sometimes, you would like to say I will never deal with this guy again, but our market is so small that sometimes you need to wipe the slate clean and forget about small disputes" (Robert). In case of default by previously trusted partners, firms generally choose to revert to "cash and carry" or "secured" transactions until debts are paid and "trust" is rebuilt.

The Importance of Relationships

Traditional solutions for limiting or eliminating contractual risk are of limited relevance in Dakar. Intense competition from both smaller and larger firms often forces SMEs to take more risks than they would like in order to "win the deal". In addition, the small size of the local market and firms' limited access to external markets in which they can get the supplies they need or sell their products severely limit the pool from which they can choose their partners. The dependence of Dakar SMEs on their suppliers and clients means that they are unlikely to be in a position to "sanction" a defaulting partner by ending the relationship. Moreover, in Dakar, the order of things can change fast and in unexpected directions. A firm in a difficult position today might become one's best partner in the near future. In such a context, severing business ties is not a decision that can be made lightly. The "shadow of the future" is almost always present, and business transactions are better understood not as discrete events, but as episodes punctuating longer business relationships.

For many interviewees, the desire to preserve future relationships with their partners played an important role in the choice of disputing strategies. Data indicate that the contractual flexibility exhibited by interviewees partly derives from their belief that suppliers and clients would take their business elsewhere if they pressed too much for enforcement. Adopting a flexible, rather than confrontational, attitude was often described as essential in order to allow the parties to remain on good terms and do business together again in the future. It remains unclear whether this belief is backed by experience, since none of the firms met mentioned having actually lost a partner because of a confrontational or inflexible attitude. Saliou, who had worked for a foreign firm with a reputation for being thorough on collection matters before starting his own business, mentioned that this experience forced him to reconsider his views on this matter: "when I was working for this other firm, I brought people to court and it had no impact on our business relationships; so if I needed to do the same now, I would not hesitate". This is consistent with the fact that firms and individuals do not always have the option to switch to a more accommodating partner without incurring additional costs. As Jacques mentioned, "if someone needs what I sell, he's going to buy from me even if he doesn't like me. And if he can buy from my competitor at a better price, he will buy from him, no matter how nice I am." In addition, a viable strategy for defaulting clients who actually have many options is to diversify their sources of supply, a measure that enables them to resist claims. In such cases, being flexible only reduces one's chance of getting paid, without bringing any benefit. As Yacine, who heads a firm in a very competitive sector, said: "the more credit you give, the more clients you lose."

Even if the pursuit of a claim does not necessarily impact on the business relationship between the parties, many of the firms met expressed some concern about the impact of their disputing behavior on their business reputation, and thus on their relationships with other partners. Going to court or pursuing claims too aggressively rather than compromising might position one as "too tough" and strict in business matters, and runs the risk of driving away existing or potential partners: "If you are really strict, people will label you as someone who might not be there to support them if need be" (Saliou). In this respect, it is important to note that, although business networks constitute the main conduits of information on firms, they also overlap with a variety of social networks based on diverse types of ties. The porous boundaries between the different kinds of networks, as well as the fact that business partners often share membership of one or more non-business networks, allow information to flow easily from one circle to another. In the absence of clearly defined boundaries between the professional and personal spheres of life, the "reputation" of a SME is intimately related to the personal reputation of the people who own and manage it. Unsurprisingly, a large number of interviewees expressed concern about the potential impact of a decision to litigate a claim on their personal reputation and relationships. A closer look at two important aspects of the local culture will shed some light on the impact of local social norms on business disputing.

The "Culture of Compromise"

Dakarois are generally keen on seeing themselves as conflict-avoiding people for whom any matter can, and should, be resolved amicably. The local culture is widely seen as a *culture de compromis*, in which conflict calls for dialogue until an agreement is reached. Litigation, which turns relationships based on negotiation for mutual gain into matters of right and wrong, is often viewed as a personal attack on the defendant's probity and entailing the destruction of all personal and professional relationships between the parties. As such, it is generally seen in a negative light, as disruptive of collective order. This perception is possibly fed by a certain tendency, common among laypeople as well as the firms met, to associate courts with the application of penal sanctions. For many, it seems that putting courts in charge of an issue, even in civil matters, automatically opens the door to the possibility of seeing one party to the dispute "condemned" and brought to prison.

The impact of the local culture of compromise on business disputing behavior does not seem insignificant, but remains hard to assess. On the one hand, the application of the obligation of compromise seems to depend on the type of relationships between the parties, and more particularly on the structure of the common networks to which they belong. In addition, general agreement on elements of the "local culture" does not prevent the existence of possible discrepancies between what Dakarois say about their preferences and what they actually do. Some were quick to point to newspaper reports of litigated cases as evidence that the place had indeed turned into a haven for lawyers, or to describe litigation as a standard and well-accepted practice in business matters. Social norms nevertheless appear to impact on a certain proportion of managers' decisions, through either internalization or social pressure. For some, preserving harmonious relationships is a priority even when it means giving up on a rightful claim. For Cheik, "I am Senegalese; those values are part of me. I feel better when I am on good terms with people, that's what makes me happy. Maybe it's a weakness, but that's the way I live." The fear of being stigmatized if one brings a case to court also plays a role in some cases: "We're not in Europe, where business is business. If you take someone to court here, all your relatives will see you in a different light" (Thierno).

"Le relationnel"

The role played by local norms favoring negotiation and compromise in business decisions cannot be properly understood without considering the specific ways in which social pressure is exerted in Dakar, through a local practice, often referred to as "mediation" or "intermediation". Dakar mediation consists in asking third parties to intervene in bilateral processes of business negotiation, by serving as an informal link between two parties unable to reach an agreement. The type of informal "mediation" in which these third parties engage is quite different from the standard definition of the term. Dakar "mediators" are not neutral third parties. As Jacques specifies, "mediation is not about finding a compromise, it's about making the other person listen to reason." Although one aspect of the role of mediators is to facilitate communication and negotiation between the parties, their essential task is to "convince" one party to behave in a certain manner.

A good proportion of interviewees indicated that they resort to their own *relationnel* in business matters, mostly in order to meet with potential clients and suppliers, but also for contract enforcement purposes. Mediators can be used to make contact with specific persons in big bureaucracies, in the hope that the creation of a personalized relationship within the firm would make it more likely to get orders or speed up payments. A well-chosen mediator may also help convince someone to pay a debt, grant further delay, or settle a claim for less than he would have otherwise. Depending on the situation, mediators can thus either contribute to the enforcement of a contract or, to the contrary, deter a party from pursuing such enforcement.

Finding a mediator willing to intercede in one's favor does not seem to require much effort in Dakar. Due to the small size of the city and the density of local networks, any two persons' circles of relations almost always overlap, making it relatively easy to find someone who knows the other party well enough to agree to intervene in a dispute. Mediators have influence not because they refer to new arguments not previously invoked by the parties themselves, but because the weight of an argument depends on the identity of the person who utters it: "moral" arguments may contain implicit threats when voiced by people in a position to exert reputational or other sanctions. On the other hand, refusing to compromise and grant the favor asked for by the mediator may have an impact on one's relationship with the mediator as well as one's reputation. As Idrissa puts it:

> this is also a matter of social acceptance: if X asked me for a favor and I said no, this would not be acceptable. If you do that, maybe tomorrow people will turn away from you and stop doing business with you, because you said no to X.

The best mediators are persons to whose opinion the other party is particularly sensitive for a variety of reasons, including the depth of their relationship with the defaulting party and their personal status. Interestingly, the special authority conferred on some religious, ethnic, or "extended family" figures, and the corresponding obligation to comply with their requests, were specifically mentioned by only a handful of the people met, all but one being of non-Senegalese origins. This may be either because non-Senegalese interviewees overestimated the influence of such persons and their role in the mediation process, or because Senegalese interviewees failed to make explicit mention of this factor because of its taken-for-granted quality.

The practice of mediation represents both an advantage and a drawback for firms. As Robert indicates:

> whatever you do here, it always ends up having an impact on someone with whom you are related in one way or another. So it is actually quite difficult to pressure someone: the guy will always find someone who knows you and who will pay you a visit.

One means to prevent the intervention of third parties in one's affairs consists in avoiding doing business with people who are "too close" to be sued and privileging arm's-length partners. This is a strategy that Idrissa uses on a regular basis:

> I tend to avoid dealing with friends, or the friends of my friends, whenever I can. Because if a problem occurs, I won't have any means to put pressure on them. So I try to come up with some reasons, I say that we are not available, or that we do not do this kind of work.

However, the overlapping of networks, which create invisible links between seemingly unrelated persons, severely limits the capacity of firms to cut themselves off from potentially problematic relations.

In addition to their role as mediators, relations also intervene in business disputes as providers of funds. In Dakar, certain kinds of relationships give rise to financial obligations to give or lend money in times of need. A debtor facing a ruthless creditor may thus try to settle a dispute by asking someone in his circle of relations to give or lend the amount at stake. These financial obligations are not restricted to relationships between relatives and may be found in a variety of more or less intimate relationships, including, as the following example shows, between suppliers and clients:

> In business, the client is always more or less a friend; we develop friendly relations with our clients. If I have a client who has been ordering from me for five years, all his clothes and his wife's clothes come from my shop, I don't even need to see him: if I know he's been arrested for 50,000 francs, I will go pay for him, because he's a friend. Someone who's been your client for five years, bringing you 2–3 million in revenues, you can intervene (Babacar).

The "friendship" described in this case was not based on personal relations beyond the business context of the relationship, and is hardly distinguishable from financial interest in the preservation of a relation.

The existence of financial obligations among related people entails that money received in payment of a debt does not necessarily come from the debtor's pocket. In such a context, aggressive claiming and litigation may have unexpected consequences. Aicha describes a case where the constraints she applied on a debtor spread to the debtor's circle of relations, to eventually reach one of her close friends, who agreed to pay in place of the debtor:

> It is only well after the fact that my friend told me about it. If he had told me from the start that he would be the one paying this debt, maybe I would have behaved differently, because of my relationship with him. I am glad he did not tell me beforehand: that's how I managed to get paid.

The important role played by third parties in the resolution of business disputes suggests that, in Dakar, conflicts are likely to transcend the limits of private bilateral relationships and take on a public character. In this respect, it is important to note that the very identity of the persons called on to intervene, and more particularly the fact that the ties they share with the parties pre-exist the birth of the conflict, plays a fundamental role in justifying their involvement in the dispute. Mediators are not considered "strangers" to the dispute, and their intervention therefore does not in itself turn the dispute into a public matter in the same way as litigation would do. From this perspective, the formal arbitration and mediation mechanisms promoted by OHADA and the local Chamber of Commerce seem more similar to litigation than to local mediation practices. For Alassane, e.g. having both parties sit in front of a mediator or arbitrator is a process of a fundamentally different nature than the involvement of the *relationnel*:

> Having three people discussing in a room, it never happens. That would mean that what we have is an open conflict. In labor relations, you can see that, but not in commercial relations, it is very rare; I have never had a case where we did have a mediator sit with us ... If you need someone to put the pieces back together, this is what I call an open conflict.

In other words, whereas resorting to the *relationnel* does not impact on the "closed" character of a dispute, using alternative dispute resolution mechanisms based on the intervention of neutral third parties entails a formal recognition that a conflict exists and needs resolution. Even resorting to formal mediation might thus signal a lack of commitment to the "culture of compromise". From this perspective, it might not be surprising to see Dakarois make very little use of the formal ADR mechanisms at their disposal.

The Emergence and Transformation of Disputes: Contractual Breach as a Fact of Life

Dakar's legal sphere is characterized by the presence of a high number of problems that could be addressed by legal means but fail to reach the forum designed to solve them. As mentioned above, a variety of factors specific to Dakar and the situation of SMEs may account for this situation. In order to better understand how these and other factors interact and impact on the management of contractual disputes in Dakar, it is necessary to take a closer look at the disputing process as a whole, and examine how disputants manage or fail to solve their problems without the intervention of courts.

In a seminal article, Felstiner, Abel and Sarat (1980) proposed that injurious experiences get (or fail to get) transformed into disputes following a three-stage process. The *naming* stage involves perceiving the experience as injurious. The next step (*blaming*) consists in the transformation of the experience into a grievance against an individual or social entity. The *claiming* stage corresponds to the voicing of the grievance to the party held responsible. Rejection of the claim leads to the emergence of a dispute *per se*.

Reacting to a particular situation first involves identifying this situation as something calling for some form of response. In other words, the situation has to be seen as out of the ordinary, and it must be possible to remedy it. Personal expectations thus play a fundamental role in determining how different people react to similar situations and their propensity to qualify an event or situation as problematic. A number of contextual factors also impact on one's expectations and perceptions: a behavior seen as perfectly normal in situation X may be perceived as an instance of gross misconduct in situation Y. The violation of a contract thus does not necessarily constitute a wrong calling for retribution.

When questioned about the problems they most frequently faced in the course of their business relationships, many of the firms met in Dakar first indicated that they never or very rarely encountered such issues. Their answers were very different, though, when the conversation referred rather to specific instances of breach (e.g. which proportion of all of your clients usually pay on time? do you usually get your orders on time?) or the "difficulties" that firms are likely to encounter in their daily activities, in which cases contract enforcement issues were described as commonplace. What sets Dakar firms apart is thus not the absence of what would qualify as "contractual breaches" in a Western context, but their failure to spontaneously mention and label such injurious experiences as "problematic" and worthy of mentioning.

A common way to account for this situation consists in pointing to some elements characteristic of "African cultures" and management styles, commonly described as "fatalistic, resistant to change, reactive, short-termist, authoritarian, risk reducing, context dependent, and basing decisions on relationship criteria, rather than universalistic criteria" (Jackson 2004, 15). In his study of contract enforcement in Ghana, Fafchamps (1996) makes a strong case against this view. Noting the low levels of contractual discipline prevailing among the firms studied, he identifies as its root cause the "low level of economic development and the magnitude of shocks to which manufacturing firms are subjected" (Fafchamps 1996, 428). The data gathered in Senegal provides support for this position. An overwhelming majority of the firms met deplored the frequency of instances of late or non-payment, order cancellation, and late or defective deliveries and acknowledged the negative consequences of such events on their business operations. Most also were aware that such events constitute contract violations that can be addressed through legal means. Their reluctance to describe such events as constituting "problems" or evidencing the existence of a "conflict" with a business partner does not appear to relate to a loose attitude toward contractual commitment but as deriving from the very prevalence of those issues. In view of the frequency of contractual problems, contract violations are closer to a "fact of life" with which one has to deal than an exceptional event.

In order to distinguish those "facts of life" that will remain so from those that will be "named" and elevated to the status of actual problems to be dealt with, it is essential to consider the close relationship between the "naming" and "blaming" stages of the disputing process. "Naming" is not only contingent on the perception of the injurious character of an event, but on the cause of such injury. Having themselves to deal with a series of unpredictable contingencies on a regular basis, firms operating in Dakar generally consider contractual compliance to be an ideal out of reach of their partners as well as themselves. In consequence, they have come to treat contractual breach as a mostly inevitable event and not to expect strict compliance with contractual terms. For them, contractual terms seem closer to an ideal than a list of precise obligations to be fulfilled at all costs. In such a context, firms are reluctant to blame their partners for every single failure to comply. Only those events for which someone is to blame will constitute actual injuries, rather than common inconveniences one has to learn to expect and deal with.

Their qualification of specific instances of breach as problems, and firms' reactions to such breaches, depends on the definite sense they gradually come to ascribe to a series of events comprising, but not limited to, the actual breach of contract. In order to understand the diverse reactions of firms facing contractual violations, it is necessary to have a closer look at how they ascribe responsibility for breach in diverse instances of contractual violation. The situations in which a contract may be violated may be classified in four main categories, based on the cause they are attributed to.

A first category comprises instances of "real dishonesty", in which individuals or firms act in bad faith and have no intention to comply. Such cases are generally considered exceptional. The other three categories concern cases in which compliance is delayed rather than simply avoided. One of them comprises those cases of default that result from events considered to be beyond the control of the defaulting party. In the case of small firms or individuals, such events may include financial or other difficulties related to the limited level of their resources. Debtors in such situations are held to be temporarily or, if bad luck persists, permanently unable to satisfy their obligation, despite their willingness to do so. Because most SMEs are exposed to risks of this type, they generally do not blame their partners for their incapacity in such cases. They nevertheless expect them to fulfill their obligations as soon as the circumstances make it possible. Another category of breaches comprises those that are attributed to issues originating from within the firm, such as internal bureaucratic hurdles or "management problems" that prevent firms from fulfilling their obligations in an appropriate and/or timely manner. Degrees of tolerance for such kind of "problems" are variable. While, in the case of very large firms or public institutions, bureaucratization and inefficiency may be seen as a correlate of firm size, problems may also be attributed to "bad habits" and inefficient modes of organization within firms. In all cases, however, default remains excusable as long as good faith is not in issue. The next category of cases concerns those situations where the defaulting party willfully chooses to delay the satisfaction of its contractual obligations for financial gain, for example by postponing the payment of bills in order to "play with the credit" granted by its suppliers. The use of such business tactics, although seen as reprehensible, is generally not held to be dishonest or to constitute fraud.

According to the firms met, claims are made in almost all cases of breach. Many mentioned that they not only make claims, but give up asking for compliance only where it is in fact impossible, where very small amounts of money are at stake, or where the costs to be incurred exceed the amounts that could be recovered. However, reactions to instances of contractual breach also evidence very high levels of flexibility among SMEs, without any significant differences between the cases where inability is due to external shocks and those where it derives from a supplier's limited financial and other resources (including limited professional and management skills). The standard response to requests for further delay to comply is to welcome them with resignation and understanding. Claimants generally give the defaulting party the benefit of the doubt as well as some time to get back on its feet. New payment schedules or other arrangements are routinely agreed upon, without interest being charged. Similarly, defective work rarely leads to claims for performance or damages. In many cases, flexibility might be the only option with the potential of offering solutions without negatively impacting on business. Flexible negotiations allow parties to find a mutually acceptable solution to what has become a common problem. Moktar, who heads a firm in the construction industry, provided the following example:

> The other day, this subcontractor told me, "I need you to pay me now, because my workers need cash to come to work tomorrow." Some workers live two hours away from the construction site, so, had I said no, they would not have come to work. This is the kind of problem we have to deal with every day.

Flexible negotiations can sometimes be assimilated to a form of partial "lumping", with firms either paying for defective work at full price, or giving extra money to correct defects. All the cases of this nature concerned small, vulnerable suppliers, who were hardly in a position to provide monetary or other types of compensation:

> even when I'm not satisfied, I pay anyway, because [these suppliers] have very limited means, I don't want to penalize them. That's why. They don't earn very much, so … even if it means I need have someone else redo the work. But I would never refuse to pay (Robert).

According to Felstiner, Abel and Sarat, disputes emerge when a claim made is rejected by the party to which it is addressed: "[d]elay that the claimant construes as resistance is just as much a rejection as is a compromise offer (partial rejection) or an outright refusal" (Felstiner, Abel and Sarat 1980, 636). Under this view, most of the claims made in Dakar would be held to generate disputes. However, the fact that perfect compliance is rarely expected and that parties are given some leeway with respect to the satisfaction of their obligations makes it harder to determine at which point a claim is considered rejected and transforms into a dispute. It could be argued that disputes start where flexibility stops, i.e. at that point where one party feels justified to stop "trying to understand" and resort to more assertive modes of claiming.

This transition from modes of claiming based on flexible negotiation to a logic of dispute resolution usually takes place when one starts seeing a breach as due to "unwillingness" to comply rather than inability. As Thierno explains, "if someone is in trouble, you have no choice but to wait. But if it is someone who has the money but refuses to pay, then war is declared." But, although it is easy to conceptualize in theory, the boundary between "faulty" and "involuntary" instances of contractual breach is far from clear in practice. The actual reasons why a party failed to comply often remain impossible to identity for outsiders. Similarly, deducting the state of mind and intentions of the other party from the behavior exhibited after the fact is not a straightforward process. Resistance to increasing pressure to comply may be interpreted both as a sign that inability is real ("if he had the money he would have paid already") and as evidence of unwillingness to pay. Ascribing a precise meaning to such behavior thus requires taking into account additional relevant elements. The interest or absence of interest in pursuing the relationship manifested by the party will often be determinant in this respect. For example, Bassirou, a distributor, indicated that his preferred strategy first involved interrupting sales to clients in default for a two-month period. Failure to pay during this period is then interpreted as evidence that the client has found a new supplier and thus ended the relationship, justifying legal action. Similarly, "good faith" debtors are expected to react to requests for compliance in a way evidencing their willingness to comply eventually. It is essential to be open about one's situation as well as to show respect and care about one's partners: one needs to take steps to find a compromise solution, keep one's word, keep lines of communication open, and minimize the impact of their breach on their partners.

Although unwillingness to comply may be inferred from the identity of the party, with larger, well-established firms being more likely to be held to their commitment, in most cases, concluding that a case is one of unwillingness comes at the end of a longer process. Wronged parties generally adopt a bilateral and gradual approach to claiming, with requests becoming more insistent and frequent as time goes by. Initial claims are generally made verbally, often over the phone, and more akin to gentle "reminders" than formal requests. Visits to the debtor's workplace or place of residence may then be made. Statements of account, reminder letters and formal notices may be sent. Diverse ways to "put pressure" on debtors may also be used. Threatened or actual suspension or termination of business relationships is sometimes used to discipline negligent suppliers, usually in competitive industries where the business relationship is more valuable to the supplier than to the client. In contrast, firms who have few alternative options will sever business relationships only in extreme cases, where the possibility of future interaction has been discarded, as in clear cases of dishonesty or lack of respect. In this case, ending the relationships is purely preventive and serves no enforcement purposes. In cases of non-payment, reverting to "cash and carry" or "secured" transactions until debts are paid is preferable to severing the relationship. Such a strategy not only allows new sales to take place, but also increases the probability of recovering the amounts owed. As Jacques explains, when money is owed,

> every new order is paid cash, and they pay also part of their debt at the same
> time. Whereas if I said "you can't buy from me until I am paid in full", they
> would not pay faster and I would not sell anything in the meantime.

Another common way to pressure debtors, and thus assess their capacity and willingness to comply, involves the intervention of third parties. Although a few of the firms met indicated that they preferred to keep discussions at the bilateral level, many mentioned regularly asking people from their *relationnels* to intervene in their business disputes. Alternatively, pressure may be applied by threatening to damage a business reputation. Abdoulaye reports: "I often tell them that Dakar is not New York – reputation matters: if you don't pay me, I will not hesitate to give you bad publicity". Financial institutions sometimes resort to a similar practice consisting in posting "mug shots" of their defaulting clients on their doors. A manager of such an institution described the practice as very effective.

A very small proportion of interviewees mentioned involving "strangers" in their dispute. A few indicated that they sometimes hire bailiffs to deliver letters or prepare official reports in order to put additional pressure on debtors. Only one of the firms involved in the study mentioned resorting regularly to the police in order to get its money back. This particular case seems exceptional in that the head of the firm in question admitted being on good personal terms with many police chiefs. In such contexts, police officers may be more akin to members of the *relationnel* with special powers of persuasion than to public officers exercising their duty. Four other instances of police intervention were mentioned. Two of them concerned a case of fraud and a NSF cheque, respectively. The other cases concern Cheik, who resorted to the police twice, in order to scare debtors: one of his debtors paid before the actual intervention of the police, while the other ended up in prison, at which point Cheik withdrew his complaint:

> I withdrew it because, well, this guy was just like me; he is young, he's in business, he bought stuff from me and it did not work out for him. He has a wife and kids. He spent two days in prison and did not pay: that means he does not have the money.

Only one interviewee indicated having resorted to collection agencies and was not satisfied with the results, and one mentioned considering the possibility of doing it in the future.

Finally, although firms who want to know about their rights when facing a dispute sometimes consult lawyers, legal professionals seem very unlikely to be asked to make representations on behalf of their clients. The general trend seems to be for lawyers to get involved at the stage where disputes have escalated and the decision to litigate has already been made. From then on, claims are handled exclusively by the lawyers in charge.

The Implicit Dimensions of Dakar Contracts

The fact that an overwhelming majority of Dakar business disputes are solved through informal mechanisms raises the question of the role that the local legal and judicial systems actually play, or could play, in the ordering of business relationships. It is worth noting that the high levels of flexibility exhibited by the interviewees in the enforcement of their agreements do not entail a total disinterest in the form and content of their business contracts. In fact, a majority of the firms involved in the study indicated that they do not content themselves with verbal agreements but resort to some other kind of written documentation, including invoices and order forms, in most of their transactions. In addition, a significant proportion of the interviewees mentioned involving lawyers or other legal professionals in the preparation of their more complex business contracts, or asking them to review the agreements prepared by their partners before signing them.

The possibility of obtaining judicial enforcement of the contract or protection from opportunistic behavior does not constitute the main reason accounting for such a resort to written documentation and lawyers. In only a few cases did the interviewees specifically express concerns with the enforceable or deterrent character of their contracts or choose to incorporate clauses serving these purposes. The perceived inability of judicial sanctions to deter breach as well as the widespread belief that the overwhelming majority of cases of breach are involuntary – and thus would occur notwithstanding the presence of harsher judicial sanctions – might account for this situation. In this context, the priority when negotiating contracts is to prevent those cases of breach that can be prevented and limit the impact of the others on business operations. This may entail taking the possibility of late delivery into account in one's planning; giving detailed specifications about the work to be done, the product to be delivered, and the schedule to be respected; and delaying full payment until satisfactory delivery, both as an incentive to comply and as a way to limit losses in case the relationship ends and a new supplier has to be found.

The written contracts made by Dakar SMEs are not generally held to state all the obligations undertaken by the parties. They are better understood as partial descriptions of the parties' expectations, additional terms being spelled out verbally or even left implicit. Such unwritten terms may complement the contract, as when detailed, written specifications about the product to be delivered combine with an informal duty (and right) of the client to monitor the supplier's work and progress. As Moktar, who operates in the construction industry, indicates: "it is our responsibility to monitor the subcontractors; if we just let them do the job and they don't do it right, we cannot charge them for the extra costs." Unwritten terms may also contradict contractual provisions, as, e.g. when parties develop new understandings of their mutual obligations as their relationships develop. In consequence, the role played by contractual provisions in business relations cannot be fully understood without taking a closer look at the informal terms actually applied by the parties in the specific context of their business relationships.

In light of the diverse conditions in which Dakar SMEs operate, it is not surprising to see that the business relationships they establish do not form a unique category in which law has a pre-determined and uniform role to play. Care should be taken, however, not to overlook the complexity of business in Dakar by resorting to doubtful, although popular, dichotomies such as the opposition between the informal and the formal sectors. In fact, many of the SMEs involved in the study described themselves as neither traditional "informal" firms, nor typical modern or formal firms adhering to models of business relationships labeled as "Western", "professional", "objective", or "legal". Data also suggest that, although the level and type of trust between the parties has an impact on their use of legal mechanisms, it would be over simplistic to categorize their business relationships as either "law-" or "trust-based". It is proposed that they could be better described as constituting a continuum ranging from, at one end, relationships hardly distinguishable from the social relations that underlie them, to, at the other end, the kind of impersonal relations established by large organizations.

In addition, although certain characteristics of firms undoubtedly have an impact on their attitudes toward law and propensity to resort to it, it would be inappropriate to assume that such characteristics determine or limit the type of relationships that firms can establish. Firms operating "informally" may be less prone to resort to legal enforcement mechanisms and more likely to rely on trust and informal solutions; however, this situation does not seem to derive from their informal status but from the nature of the business relationships they tend to develop. Very small firms, which form the bulk of the informal sector, are more likely to depend on personal relations to develop their business, especially where, as in Dakar, access to external credit is limited or inexistent. This seems particularly true with respect to the informal traders that form part of the Murid distribution networks, which provide access to goods and credit in addition to serving important social functions. Traders belonging to such networks are therefore unlikely to make a clear distinction between the norms governing their social relations and those applicable in business matters. And yet, it does not mean that they are unable to or are uninterested in developing other kinds of business relationships in other contexts.

Keeping these reservations in mind, it is suggested that a useful way to shed light on the nature and diversity of Dakar business relationships consists in categorizing them in terms of their position on the above-mentioned "social–legal" continuum. Three main categories of relationships then emerge, corresponding to the two ends and the middle range of the continuum. These three ideal types do not purport to be mutually exclusive and describe the whole range of Dakar contractual relations. They are used primarily because of their potential contribution to building a better understanding of the logics governing these relations as well as the diverse functions played by law in the business transactions taking place in Dakar.

Business Contracts as Social Relations

A first type of business contracts comprises those business relations essentially regulated by social norms hardly distinguishable from those applying to non-business relationships. Mostly verbal and governed by "trust", those contracts are established on the basis of pre-existing business or non-business ties between members of a relatively close-knit network. People in such relationships do not establish a clear separation between the "personal" and "business" sides of their activities, and tend to incorporate non business considerations in their business decisions. They generally describe themselves as peaceful persons, and are of the view that all problems can be solved amicably if one tries hard enough. They are mostly concerned with the preservation of harmonious relationships with their partners, as well as with the members of the larger networks to which they belong. The preservation of one's reputation as an honest businessperson and a decent human being is primordial.

In such contracts, informal, collective understandings of what constitutes appropriate behavior generally come to supersede written contractual clauses or the verbal agreements reached by the parties. The high levels of flexibility that characterize those contracts are primarily the expression of the collective values of tolerance, understanding and solidarity that govern all intra-network social encounters. Law plays a marginal role in such agreements.

Problems encountered in the course of those contracts are solved exclusively through non-confrontational means. Conflicts are resolved within the network and resorting to external third parties is discouraged as disruptive of collective order. Social pressure and potential damages to one's reputation constitute the main reasons for avoiding litigation. Multilateral reputation mechanisms play a major role in the resolution of disputes. Resort to the parties' *relationnel* is common. In view of the profound embeddedness of those contracts within social networks, the relative positions of the parties in such networks is key to understanding the power dynamics at play in their relationship. Parties with more relational resources are at an advantage when time comes to press the other party to behave in their interests.

Although resorting to social contracts might require some degree of personal commitment to social norms of solidarity and compromise, it does not prevent parties from questioning the adequacy of such norms in a business context. Many interviewees involved in this kind of relationships recognized that the lack of a clear separation between the personal and business spheres of their lives, and the use of social pressure to enforce social norms of flexibility, compromise, and solidarity in business matters, could constitute important impediments to the profitability and development of their businesses. As Thierno mentions, "the problem we have here is that we always mix business and family matters". Credit must sometimes be extended notwithstanding one's ability to repay. The importance put on "trust" also makes it likely that risk management mechanisms such as asking for a banker's draft or signing an agreement will be seen as evidence of unwarranted wariness.

With vigorous continuing attempts to "formalize" informal traders as well as the collapse and dismantlement of many business empires associated with the "informal model" of business development in recent years and the increasing (although partial) formalization of some of the most important players of the informal sector, one might wonder what the future of this business model will be. Although business contracts based on social networks are unlikely to disappear any time soon, it is probable that other models will gradually come to penetrate their current strongholds, through increased exposure to alternative modes of functioning or a more acute understanding of the constraints it may place on firms' competitiveness. For example, Idrissa, an entrepreneur in his sixties, mentions:

> when I started in business, I was feeling very ill at ease with all this, the impact of family values, cultural values, and whatnot. But you always end up paying the piper … I think that those among us whose firms managed to survive longer understand the limits that you need to put on subjectivity if you want your business to grow.

The case of Lamine, who heads two distinct firms in the trade sector, shows that it is possible for a single person to develop many different types of business relationships. Lamine first followed the classic route of many informal traders. Belonging to a family of informal entrepreneurs, he spent a few years abroad trying to get ahead in international trade, before going back to Senegal. Unwilling to engage in activities that would put him in competition with his older brothers, he developed a new line of business based on the design and import of an exclusive line of clothing and involving the use of quite sophisticated formal contracts. In parallel, he also operates a food distribution business whose activities are based essentially on verbal contracts formed with members of his original social network. He describes his experience in the following terms:

> In 1982–83, I was at Sandaga's,[1] what we call the school of *informel*; everywhere in the world you find people who were trained at Sandaga. Back then, I was young, I wanted to become just like one of those rich traders I saw around. But these people only got ahead because they were lucky: they did not know anything. All of them, all my models, they went bankrupt. I think at some point, if you want to reach a certain level, you need to know the law and use it. What I owe you should not depend on my good will.

Business Contracts as Partnerships

The second type of business contracts observed in Dakar consists in primarily bilateral relationships between two parties seeing themselves as "partners" in business. The categorization of a relationship as a partnership depends on the implicit norms perceived to be governing the relationship in question. Partnership

---

1   Sandaga's market, the largest market in Dakar, constitutes the trading business hub of the Murid Islamic order.

relationships may emerge between related as well as unrelated parties, to the extent that a certain level of trust has been built, generally in the course of business.

"Partnerships" are defined primarily in contrast to profit-driven market exchanges. They are understood to entail obligations such as risk-sharing, mutual support, trust, and respect. They nevertheless have a clear instrumental function. Parties in partnership contracts are primarily concerned with the survival and development of their business, which often depends on the preservation of cooperative relationships with major partners. In view of their fragility and the number of contingencies they face, they put a high value on the ability to count on the support of their business partners in times of trouble.

Partnerships exhibit high levels of contractual flexibility, both as a means to preserve valued relationships and as a form of insurance in case of trouble. Displays of understanding entitle one to expect the same kind of behavior from others in times of need. For example, Saliou, who sells supplies to both public and private institutions, talked about the former in the following terms:

> They often have problems with their budget, so we need to help them. They see
> us as partners, not only people who want to make money with them, but real
> partners. So when we get in trouble, they manage to find some money for us so
> that we can pay our own suppliers and keep on working together.

In case of problems, partners deal with them according to their interpretation of the behavior of the other party. Pressure is applied, including through one's *relationnel*, partly in order to ascertain whether the other party should still be seen as a partner with an interest in the relationship or not. Although litigation remains an option for dealing with non-partners, it is generally excluded on the basis of cost–benefit calculations.

Partnership contracts often combine written clauses and informal business norms, the latter tending to take precedence over the former as time passes. By clarifying the expectations of the contracting parties, written terms prevent disagreements from occurring, thus contributing to the preservation of the relationship. For example, written contracts may be valuable in preventing order cancellation. By asking for commitments to be put in writing, one increases the probability that one's partners will feel too embarrassed to change their minds or invoke "mistakes" in the placement or processing their orders in order to escape from their obligations, or that they will offer some form of compensation in return for cancelling their order.

Signing a contract does not guarantee that the other party will satisfy his obligations or even act in good faith, and provides no particular protection against opportunism. Some minimal level of trust is thus prerequisite to entering into any kind of contract exceeding a certain level of risk: "there are some people I would never work with, even with a nice, signed contract, I would not; because they don't keep their promises" (Abdoulaye). Yet, agreeing to sign a contract constitutes an undisputable indication that one has deliberately agreed to assume an obligation. The use of written documents as signs of commitment varies with the level of trust between the parties to a relationship. Contracts between trusting partners are often prepared and signed after the parties have started to fulfill their obligations. In contrast, where trust is only partial, requiring one's partners to commit in writing allows one to distinguish real commitments from potentially empty promises.

Parties involved in partnerships are unlikely to blame their partners for their failure to comply, and generally readily agree to adjust their demands toward the other party when circumstances require. Requests for flexibility or compliance are generally uttered in moral rather than legal terms, with the emphasis being put on one's own needs and problems rather than one's rights and the correlative obligations of the other party. As Abdoulaye, who heads a small firm in a competitive sector of the service industry, indicated, "you have to be careful when you approach a client. For example, if a client hasn't paid a bill, I may call him and tease him a bit, saying something like 'I guess you forgot me, I am not in your planning for the day'". From this perspective, written clauses may have little impact on one's propensity to comply, but nevertheless present the important advantage of providing parties with a clear basis upon which future negotiations are to take place: the presence of written clauses makes it clear for both parties that flexibility in their application is a favor calling for immediate or future retribution

Although they do not erase power differentials, partnership contracts seem to even out inequalities somewhat. Because of their emphasis on mutual support and reciprocity, they tend to benefit the weaker party to a relationship, with stronger parties feeling an obligation to refrain from taking advantage of their position and support their partners in need. For example, Issa mentioned that, even though the sand market is a very competitive one, he had been dealing with the same supplier, an informal individual enterprise, for many years. He described their relationship in the following terms:

> We've worked together since 1991. We had problems only once, during the *hivernage*, he did not stock enough to prevent a shortage, so we played though and we stopped ordering from him, then he made up for it and we haven't had any problem since … It can take 4–5 deliveries before we tell him to come get his money, but never more than that; because we know he could get into trouble. And when he needs money and he comes to us, then we pay right away.

Business Contracts as Legal Agreements

A third conception of business relationships consists in seeing them as series of distinct transactions between independent parties. These contracts leave little or no room for flexible, *ex post* adjustment. They are thus appropriate only in cases where flexibility is not required and one's lack of understanding is unlikely to impact on the preservation of valuable relationships. Indeed, such contracts are thus more likely to be favored by firms in relatively good competitive and financial positions and having an established customer base. The advantageous position they occupy in the market and the dependence of their contractual partners toward them entail that they can get away with inflexibility and a confrontational attitude. This allows them to give priority to the profitability and development of their businesses over the creation or preservation of business relationships, and to long-term financial considerations over short-term cash flow management concerns.

Contracts of this type are generally not the product of negotiations between the parties. They are more likely to be imposed by parties in a superior bargaining position, who also determine most of the terms of the agreement. For SMEs, doing business with the state, international institutions and some domestic and foreign private firms often means agreeing to pre-set price, payment and delivery terms. As Idrissa says, "even in the private sector, with the large enterprises, might is right, you might have some leverage, but most of the time, you just accept their terms. There is just no room to maneuver."

The use of legal agreements could be seen as a way to discipline contractual partners and increase predictability. But, in view of the little impact that the presence of legal sanctions has on the frequency of contractual breach, it might be more appropriate to view resorting to such legal agreements as one aspect of a more encompassing process of specialization, bureaucratization and professionalization taking place within firms in expansion. From a management perspective, legal agreements contribute to the rationalization of firms' credit and debt-collection functions, through the standardization of contracting and claiming behavior. Standard policies and contracts are adopted, and problems are dealt with according to a pre-defined procedure, often by people external to the firm or belonging to a department distinct from the commercial branch. Such specialization allows for the establishment of a clear distinction between the people in charge of claims and collection matters and the employees who deal with the client or supplier in the normal course of the business relationships. This distinction then allows sellers or buyers to distance themselves from the claims made by other representatives of their businesses and maintain harmonious commercial relationships.

Legal agreements are meant to bind both parties and spell out the totality of their respective obligations. In practice, though, they generally apply to partners who do not have an equal access to legal remedies and tend to be eminently one-sided. Parties in a favorable market position can both afford the costs and consequences associated with litigation, and, since dependent parties will often avoid litigation and conflict at any costs, take some liberty with respect to the satisfaction of their own obligations. A few interviewees mentioned that past instances of disagreements with partners in legal relationships made them aware of the need to put the details of their contracts in writing, to plan for contingencies in their contracts, and to read carefully the contracts proposed by their partners before signing them. Saliou provided the following example: "now, I take a picture of the product, show it to the client and have him sign it. With this, if he refuses delivery, saying it is not the right product, I can show the picture to prove my point." This suggests that, even though litigation is rarely an option for firms in weak competitive positions, written contracts may constitute a useful tool for negotiating with partners more sensitive to "legal" than "relational" arguments.

Implicit Agreement ... and Disagreements: Dealing with Divergent Views

The proposed categorization of business contracts as social relations, partnerships or legal agreements is based on descriptions of what the interviewees expect from their contractual partners and how they conceive of their own obligations toward them. As subjective, individual beliefs about the norms attached to a relationship, they constitute what Rousseau (1995) calls "psychological contracts". Those subjective expectations are likely to remain implicit as long as no issue relating to their application emerges. It is thus only when disagreement about the interpretation of a norm or its relevance to a specific issue arises that parties will realize that they do not share a common understanding of the normative content of their relationship.

Although collective, shared beliefs about appropriate behavior undoubtedly impact on subjective beliefs, the decision to enter into one type of contract or another depends on a variety of factors distinct from personal values and preferences. Defining the normative content of a specific relationship is not simply a matter of conforming to personal or collective norms, but one of behaving in conformity with the rules applicable to particular situations. It involves choosing, between many different sets of expectations, the rules to be followed in the situation at play. March suggests that rule following is not grounded on cost–benefit analysis, but on a "logic of appropriateness":

> Decision makers are imagined to ask (explicitly or implicitly) three questions:
> ... What kind of situation is this? ... What kind of person am I? ... What does a

person such as I, or an organization such as this, do in a situation such as this? The process is not random, arbitrary, or trivial. It is systematic reasoning, and often quite complicated (March 1994, 58).

From this perspective, individual decisions result from the identification of the frame or role evoked by particular situations and its matching with the corresponding rules of appropriate behavior. The question then becomes one of determining which role will be taken on by the individual in the situation at play, and which set of rules will therefore apply. In relationships involving individuals linked by multiple ties of a diverse nature, individual choices about the dominant role may differ, leading to disagreements over the norms applying in the relationship. Similar divergences may also arise within organizations, whose members do not always share a single view of the nature of the relationship between the organization and outsiders. Saliou stated: "I am a tenacious person, but my employees are not; they would say 'Let the clients breathe!' I always say no. It is one of my personal flaws, I mean, they see it as a flaw: I see it as an asset." In such cases, it might be necessary for managers to work on the alignment of expectations within the organization in order to prevent potential conflicts with and between employees.

The interviews show that Dakar business actors often have divergent conceptions of the normative content of their relationships. A typical example concerns cases in which one of the parties expects his relations to be based on a social contract, while the other views it as a partnership or legal contract. In such cases, the major point of disagreement between the parties concerns the separable character of the "social" and "business" spheres of their lives, with one party deploring the encroachment of social considerations on business decisions, while being blamed as being too tough and inflexible by the other. Other cases concern relationships viewed as partnerships by one party and legal agreements by the other, leading to disagreement about the applicability of the norm of flexibility and mutual help in the relationship. This type of divergence seems more likely to occur in heavily unequal relationships where the stronger party imposes a legal frame partly foreign to the other, as well as in relationships with foreign firms or larger Senegalese businesses, which do not generally share the local understandings of the informal norms governing social relationships. Indeed, many interviewees reported a certain dissatisfaction with the "lack of trust", "insensitivity", and unwillingness to act as real partners displayed by foreign or larger firms. One of them, Cheik, recounted having put an end to a relationship for this very reason:

I used to be one of their authorized dealers, so one day I went to buy some stock, and the guy told me I had to pay right away. So I said, 'OK, I'll write you a check', but he insisted that I pay cash. I got me really mad; to me it was clearly a lack of trust. So I said: 'Things don't work this way – we defined a partnership, you asked me to pay and I accepted, but then you won't take my check?' I got very angry. Now I try to stay clear of them.

There are many ways to prevent and deal with these kinds of problems. A first one consists in selecting one's business partners on the basis of the frame they are likely to apply to the relationship. As mentioned above, one may limit the impact of social norms on their business by privileging arm's- length partners over relatives and other people whose status and *relationnel* insulate from pressure. Such strategies can be observed in a variety of industries, even the most traditional ones, as shown in Ndione's (1994) study of Dakar woodworkers, who seek to avoid social pressure and improve their bargaining position toward their apprentices by hiring "social orphans" rather than members of their networks

Another strategy consists in signaling one's views on business relations in general, in the hope that it will impact on the other party's framing of the relationship. For example, one's preference for "partnerships" over "social relations" may be signaled by minimizing the role of the parties' *relationnels* in the relationship. Abdoulaye said that he refrained from asking for a third party's intervention in order to insulate his business from external influences:

> If you ask other people to act on your behalf, then someone else can do the same in return. But if you make it clear that, in your business, you always ask people directly rather than through other people, people don't tend to come to you. It is something you can control.

More bluntly, Aicha indicated that she explicitly denies members from her *relationnel* the right to make claims on her: "I often say, 'If I were to say yes to you after saying no to this person, this would mean I am a hypocrite. There is no reason why I should be able to do something just because *you* are the one asking for it. I'm not this kind of person.'"

Parties may also engage in open negotiation over the normative content of a relationship. Aicha, who heads a SME operating in the manufacturing sector, provided a good example of such a process:

> We had an important order to fill, so we ordered 5 tons of raw materials from our supplier in France, payable on delivery. In the meantime, our client cancelled the order, so we had 5 tons of material we had no use for but still had to pay, that represented a lot of money that we did not have at that point. We needed to play tight to get our supplier to understand the situation. At one point, I told

them to take back their merchandise. I said 'There is nothing I can do. If you don't want to let us use your stuff and sell products, so that we can pay you, then you should just take it back. I won't go crazy about this. You need to understand, things like this happen, it's a case of *force majeure*, and each of us needs to play along. We've known each other for a while, we paid all your bills so far ... If an order is cancelled, I can't see how I can manage the situation. We need to split the difference and bear the burden together, I can't take everything on me; you are not taking any risks with me, I always pay for things that I can't even inspect beforehand, and nothing protects me in return, I take more risks than you, so at one point, we need to calm down and start playing by the rules.

For Aicha, the behavior of the French supplier amounted to a violation of the implicit norms of risk sharing and flexibility that were to govern their relationship and a sign of insensitivity and unwillingness to "play by the rules". Her decision to express her discontentment and state her own expectations led to a peaceful resolution of the dispute: the supplier finally agreed to deliver the supplies on credit.

However, open discussions over the norms that are to govern a relationship carry some risks. There is a danger that the parties will not be able to agree on the normative content of their relations, leading to discontent and potential relationship breakdown. In addition, firms opposing norms that are widely accepted by the other players in their industry or in the larger community to which they belong open themselves to the application of reputational sanctions. For example, although many interviewees expressed the view that social obligations should not in theory interfere with the functioning of their business, few of them seemed in a position to apply this principle in the course of all of their business relationships. For example, Ibrahima arrived one hour late to our appointment because he had to attend a religious ceremony. He explained that, even though social obligations should not, in theory, interfere in business matters, his absence from the ceremony would have been socially unacceptable, even if it took place during business hours.

Firms may avoid such difficulties by trying to limit the negative impact of specific norms in ways that do not signal a lack of commitment to those norms. This allows them to get the best of both normative worlds, by reaping the benefits of the norms favored by their partners without suffering from their disadvantages, while preserving a reputation as a valuable business "partner" and decent human being. This result can be achieved by blaming one's lack of compliance with the partner's norm on third parties or circumstances over which one has no control. In its most basic form, this strategy involves presenting one's decision as being made under external pressure, for example from bankers, suppliers asking for payment, or clients waiting for their orders. By blaming others for forcing them to be inflexible, while emphasizing their own problems and needs and asking the other party for help, firms can escape their obligations to be flexible and are able to use the norm of solidarity for enforcement purposes: "People would ask me for help, and I would say, 'I can help but only up to a certain point, because there comes a time when I am not in control anymore, when the state, or courts, or others start making demands on me'" (Idrissa).

An alternative strategy consists in voluntarily surrendering control over decisions, by delegating the responsibility for claiming to people from whom rigor and intransigence are better accepted. External service providers or even employees of the firm may be called on to make claims, thus allowing "commercial people" to preserve harmonious relationships with their contacts in other firms. For Saliou, "it is pretty simple. Your accountant sends a letter, litigates the claim and all, and once you got your money, you go back to your client and say, 'you know how accountants are, they only care for money; but what *I* want is to do business with you.'" In some cases, the fact of a manager distancing himself from how a dispute is handled by or on behalf of the firm might turn a personal affair into a dispassionate problem to be solved by professionals, thus limiting the negative impact of the conflict on the personal and commercial relations between the parties. Alassane mentioned a case in which the decision to litigate was partly made with a view to preserving a personal relationship:

> I have this childhood friend with whom I play basketball every Sunday. We had this business dispute, we could not agree on a solution, he was asking for things I didn't think he was entitled to, so each of us put his lawyer in charge and they took care of the matter. ... I remember how it happened, one night, we bumped into each other at the grocery store, and we started talking about this matter and realized we would not get along. So we both agreed to send the file to our lawyers; that's how we decided to go to court ... Rather than making things worse, we just got rid of the whole matter, and maintained the relationship we've had since we were kids.

For many interviewees, the depersonalization of business disputes seemed to represent as much a precondition for growth as a consequence of it. Serigne, a top executive at a medium-sized firm operating in the manufacturing sector, presented bureaucratization and delegation of power as explicit strategies employed by the founder of his firm, a self-made man with little formal education: although the business is still owned by its founder, it is now managed by "professionals", whose job partly consists in preventing the owner from being "exposed" to hard-to-resist claims based on social norms and isolating his business from social pressures. Similarly, Thierno, who heads a family firm, referred to his plans to turn it into a corporation (*société anonyme*) as a way to free managers from certain social constraints and allow the firm to enter a new phase of growth: "we have to take into account certain outdated parameters, because we are still a family firm. When the business becomes a corporation, it will be different, another world: professionalism, no feelings, only interests – business is business."

In this respect, it is worth noting that, although the various strategies devised by businesspeople to limit the application of local social norms may be interpreted as evidence of their limited commitment to those norms, it is not necessarily the case. In general, the interviewees tended to see the evolution of local business norms in line with dominant business models as inevitable. Their reactions to this state of affairs were quite varied, ranging from some kind of nostalgia for the good old days to a clear discontent with what they saw as the lack of professionalism of the local business community. In many cases, the adoption of "objective" or "impersonal" ways of doing business by interviewees actually seemed essentially motivated by the perceived unsuitability of the current context of local cultural norms to which they nevertheless remain deeply attached. Idrissa's description of the "culture of compromise" and its impact on business activities illustrates such ambivalence:

> Our culture is not based on sanctions. We always try to reach a compromise. That's why people are allowed to clog the streets; people are not supposed to do business on the sidewalks and all, but they do, so we have mechanics working just in front of our building. This culture of compromise, at one point, it becomes hardly bearable for everyone. ... Now, in my industry, the decisions are 80 percent based on objective factors. Because the nature of the actors, suppliers, clients, beneficiaries, does not allow for that cultural trait of compromise. ... African values are losing ground. *Les affaires à l'africaine,*[2] ten years from now, it's gone.

---

2   African management methods.

Chapter 5

The Role of Law in Business Contracts:
Lessons from Dakar

Substantial resources are devoted each year to "rule of law" and "investment climate" reforms. And yet, despite the voluminous empirical evidence now available about the relationship between development and legal institutions, little remains known about the actual impact of those reforms on social and economic life. The law and development field is still facing an important "problem of knowledge" (Carothers 2006) about the role of law and its capacity to drive economic development. By reframing the issue of the required "fit" between law and the society in which it applies as a political matter of "participation" and "ownership", policymakers have been able to eschew important questions about the very possibility of effective law reform. Under this "bookish" approach to legal change (Legrand 2001, 65), a country's success as a reformer essentially depends on the content and volume of the reforms actually implemented, with little consideration of their impact on development. In view of the little attention brought to the investigation of the consequences of the reforms implemented so far, one is left with the impression that law reform actually constitutes an end in itself, rather than a means to development.

The failure of academics and policymakers to resolve uncertainty about the validity of basic assumptions underlying the law and development approach was the main motivation for undertaking the investigation described in this book. The empirical work conducted in Dakar was designed first and foremost as a humble contribution to bridging the knowledge gap. Its objective was not to provide conclusive evidence that law reform can, or cannot, have desirable consequences in developing countries. By resorting to an inductive, qualitative approach, it rather aimed at examining fundamental, unresolved issues about the role of law and culture in economic activity and the capacity of law reform to modify business behavior.

This investigation started from the assumption that legal institutions are seldom used by SMEs operating in Dakar, and from the need to get a better understanding of the reasons accounting for this state of affairs. For this purpose, it was held necessary to examine the question of legal transplant efficiency from an interdisciplinary perspective, and to make room for a close investigation of the role of informal norms in business behavior and their relationship with formal law. In this respect, and even though they hold deeply different views about the factors that best account for human behavior, it is interesting to note that approaches focusing on economic rationality, culture or the role of trust are in agreement on one fundamental point: the notion that the absence or non-use of law implies either the absence of contracts, or the presence of other, informal, contract mechanisms conceived as functional equivalents of legal institutions. The presence, persistence and use of such institutions is then accounted for in terms of their capacity to achieve similar, or better, results than law in different circumstances and settings. For anthropologists and cross-management theorists, contract enforcement preferences are driven by specific cultural "traits" and norms, which both make litigation unattractive and provide parties with socially acceptable, non-confrontational ways to solve their disputes. For economists and economic sociologists, resorting to informal mechanisms is not culturally determined but derives from the relative efficiency of law and "community-" or "trust-based" alternatives in specific circumstances. In all cases, though, law remains the standard against which other "alternatives" are compared.

It was also noted that studies of informal norms and networks give informal mechanisms very different treatments depending on the settings in which they operate. In the case of Western countries, the combination of efficient legal institutions and high levels of "generalized trust" is said to make most transactions possible. Informal mechanisms are generally accounted for by pointing either to the inherent inability of even the most efficient courts to enforce particular types of transactions, or to the competitive advantages that firms can gain by developing "embedded ties" with their partners, particularly in industries in which information-sharing and responsiveness to change are essential. In contrast, the informal institutions found in developing countries are not conceived of as presenting specific advantages compared to formal law. Their existence is generally attributed either to the inadequacy of formal legal institutions, or to local cultural characteristics preventing people from embracing those institutions. As mere "second-best" alternatives, they are a sign of underdevelopment and destined to disappear as development takes place (or, in culturalist terms, for development to become possible). The networks found in developing countries are not conceptualized as being formed of business ties designed to achieve efficiencies, but as close-knit (non business) communities administering reputational sanctions. Those "strong ties" are said to constitute both the main source of trust in developing countries and a liability that limits business activity by erecting "barriers to entry".

The data gathered in Dakar provide important insights into the nature and role of "informal mechanisms", as well as into the strengths and weaknesses of those arguments. In this final chapter, three aspects of the literature will be discussed in light of the data, before presenting some policy and research implications of this book.

The Shadow of Law: Beyond Sanctions

Relying on transaction cost economics and game theory, the new law and development movement takes a functional perspective in which legal institutions are seen as providers of sanctions that guide behavior. In some ways, the game-theory models now in vogue may be seen as refined versions of older cost–benefit approaches in use in the "access to justice" programs of the 1970s and 80s. In both cases, legal and judicial reform aim at making courts speedier and cheaper – and legal professionals more competent and less corrupt – in order to make sanctions more salient and encourage the use of courts or alternative dispute resolution mechanisms recognized by law. But, whereas access to justice programs focused on the equality of disputants before the law, current law and development initiatives emphasize the negative economic consequences of inefficient legal institutions: where the legal system is unable to provide sanctions, transactions either do not take place, or they are supported by alternative, informal sanctioning mechanisms. By fixing "incentives" to comply, law reform favors compliance with the law and allows for the "legal security" needed for business.

The data gathered in Dakar reveal a different perspective on the impact of legal efficiency on business behavior. Few interviewees expressed concerns about judicial corruption and competence or, more generally, the lack of legitimacy of the legal and judicial system. In addition, although many were dissatisfied with the delay needed to enforce a judicial decision, one may suggest that delay in question was unreasonable mainly because of the immediacy of their need for money or supplies essential to the pursuit of their business operations. Similarly, the material costs of litigation, although not necessarily unreasonable in the abstract, may often become excessive depending on the amount at stake.

The main factor preventing the interviewed SMEs from litigating their claims had little to do with the efficiency of the system, since it concerned the impossibility of any system to recover money from insolvent or poor debtors. As to the notion that the existence of informal enforcement mechanisms may account for the little use made of law, data partly supports the notion that local social norms enforced within business or social communities have a sanctioning function in Dakar. However, it is also clear that the primary function of those norms is not to ensure compliance, but to enforce the norm of flexibility and mutual support that underlies the local "culture of compromise" and on which most firms depend.

In fact, the informal mechanisms present in Dakar may be more efficient in preventing creditors from claiming their due than in enforcing commitments.

The inductive approach taken during fieldwork shifted the focus of inquiry from the "sanctions" hypothesized to drive behavior to the actual factors on which people base their decisions, and revealed that Dakar firms' disregard for legal remedies thus cannot be accounted for by the lack of legal sanctions available or their relative inefficiency for contract enforcement compared to informal mechanisms. The interviews indicate that, for SMEs, it is the business environment prevailing in Dakar, rather the absence of sanctions, that accounts for most of the instances of contractual breach. The very factors that make contractual compliance difficult for SMEs contribute to making the court system ill-suited for the resolution of their disputes. The limited resources at the disposal of SMEs, the concomitant emphasis they put on day-to-day cash management and viability, the small size of their typical transactions, and their dependence toward their partners make litigation unattractive to them, irrespective of the actual costs and delay it would involve. In consequence, they are unlikely to engage in sophisticated evaluations of the legal or judicial system in place. The same can be said with respect to formal ARD mechanisms such as the mediation and arbitration services provided by the Centre d'Arbitrage, de Médiation et de Conciliation of the Chamber of Commerce, which, despite the important efforts deployed by the Chamber to make businesses aware of their existence and advantages, were of little interest to the vast majority of interviewees.

From this perspective, it seems that the behavior of Dakar SMEs has more to do with their structural position in the global economy than with the legal environment in which they operate. This is not to say, however, that legal factors have no impact on the decisions made during the disputing process. What is suggested is that such impact actually bears little relationship to the actual "efficiency" of the institutions in place: what matters for disputants is not so much the costs and benefits to be derived from their use as the extent to which they perceive litigation as an option, however remote, that they could consider using at some point. From this perspective, "legal efficiency" might better be seen as a dichotomous variable (efficient/inefficient) than a continuous one: the degree to which specific legal institutions are "functional" matters little, as long as they constitute a threat, however vague, for the disputants they aim to serve. The relevance of legal institutions is thus a subjective matter only partly related to objective measures of efficiency.

Assessing the Role of Culture in Business Relations

The benchmarking approach of the World Bank, which turns foreign legal institutions into models to imitate, illustrates well the limited room made for "local adaptations" in the law and development agenda. Despite claims about the need to take local conditions into account when devising reforms, the adaptations made are generally little more than marginal adjustments designed to make the laws easier to implement and apply. The widespread assumption that "rational" cost-benefit considerations, rather than cultural factors, determine economic behavior has also justified the little interest brought in the investigation of the potential role of culture in economic activity. If "business is business" all over the world, then the best business law practices are the best everywhere.

Data partly confirm the notion that culture has little role to play in business activity. Although the interviewees hardly looked like the culture-free Prisoner Dilemma's players posited by economists, cultural factors did not emerge as the main determinants of their business behavior. The attitudes they display not only reflect the reality of SMEs all over the world, but also are consistent with the well-documented tendency of businesspeople in general to pay only marginal attention to the applicable legal rules and the efficiency of the court system when making business decisions.

Yet, this book should not be interpreted as depriving "culture", however defined, of any role in business and legal matters. Many interviewees mentioned the high value attached to negotiation and compromise in Senegal as part of the "shared, collective beliefs regarding appropriate behavior in a society" (Rousseau 1995, 13) that generally govern social interactions in Dakar. When internalized, such shared beliefs impact on people's self-identity and their willingness and capacity to depart from what is generally perceived as acceptable behavior. High levels of norm internalization may make people more likely to prioritize social considerations over the profitability of their businesses and make it difficult to adopt alternative conceptions of business relations. This is particularly true in cases where business and social considerations overlap, such as small firms embedded in intricate networks of business relationships based on social ties, whose survival depends on the preservation of those ties.

Data show that the relationship between "culture" and the behavior of business actors is not as straightforward as "trait-based" theories of culture propose. The interviewees also expressed variable degrees of allegiance to local norms, and mentioned a number of strategies that they use to limit impact on their business operations. In addition, many of those who adhered to local norms were also aware of the potential negative consequences of their application in business matters on the profitability of their business, and the resulting need to redefine their business relationships in new terms in order to survive and grow. Social norms thus constitute only one of the variables influencing the process through which decisions about the behavior to adopt are made. This suggests that so-called "cultural" norms such as the ones observed in Dakar can hardly be treated as an independent variable and investigated as such.

The subjective perspective on contracts adopted in the present work provides interesting insights into the relationship between culture and business behavior and how it can be investigated. From data, shared values and beliefs may be seen to play a role at three different levels during the disputing process. First, they influence the expectations that people have towards each other and, consequently, their interpretation of each other's behavior. In this respect, it is worth noting that beliefs described as "cultural" may also be seen as deriving from the environment in which people evolve, these two factors ultimately reinforcing each other. For example, the reluctance of interviewees to use terms such as "problems", "breaches" or "conflicts" to designate events that, to the interviewer, constituted clear instances of contractual violation could thus be held as deriving from a local culture in which contractual breach is acceptable, or as a tendency not to categorize as problematic events whose occurrence is both common and expected. From this perspective, culture is not as much an "obstacle to development" as the product of specific, historical economic circumstances.

Second, cultural norms impact on one's subjective perceptions of what others consider socially acceptable. In other words, they play a role in the calculation of the reputational costs attached to specific behaviors. These costs in turn impact on people's willingness to set themselves apart from the crowd by behaving in contradiction to the norm, notwithstanding their personal levels of commitment to the norm in question. On this matter, it is worth noting that labeling a specific behavior as socially "inappropriate" is the product of subjective processes, in which one's perceptions of the person whose behavior is examined and the situation in which this person is play an important role. From this perspective, behavior can hardly be assessed independently from the motives ascribed by the observer to the person whose conduct requires justification. This is the reason why claims for payment are likely to be answered differently where they are framed in terms of personal needs for support rather than in terms of rights. To be seen as inappropriate, a specific behavior not only has to violate behavioral expectations, but also has to be impossible to justify in terms compatible with local values.

Even though "contractual flexibility" may be partly accounted for in terms of the importance of compromise in Dakar local culture, it is also clear that local norms do not provide a uniform set of expectations applying in all contexts and situations. The third role of cultural norms is to provide criteria for determining which set of expectations applies in a specific situation. As the existence of "partnership contracts" and "legal contracts" indicates, the values of compromise and solidarity identified as forming part of the Senegalese culture aim primarily at regulating relations among intimates and family members, and lose their relevance as social distance increases. Defining the normative content of a specific relationship thus entails identifying the nature of the relationship in question, through an often complex, heuristic process of categorization.

By determining what distinguish friends from strangers, relatives from relations, partners from counterparts, and equals from superiors, social norms provide metarules that allow parties to put an appropriate label on their relationship and adjust their behavior accordingly. As business relationships often evolve as the parties get to know each other and develop more intimate ties, the categorization of relationships is an on-going process. Data suggest that, in Dakar, the respective positions of the parties in the social structure have a significant impact on their framing of their relationships. An obvious example concerns the difficulty expressed by interviewees to apply "business" norms when dealing with friends or relatives, even in a business context. Even in such cases, however, a number of strategies may be used in order to allow a certain frame to prevail over the one that the parties would be expected to apply. For example, bureaucratization may be seen as a way to "reframe" personal relationships as more "impersonal" ones in which social norms do not apply, thus reducing the reputational costs attached to "anti-social" behavior. Conversely, appealing to sentiments constitutes a way for businesses to "weave obligations" (Darr 2007) in cold business relations and turn them into more personal ones, thus increasing the chances that norms of solidarity and support will ultimately prevail. Such strategic attempts to favor the application of a specific frame may have a limited impact, however, in heavily unequal relationships, where the most powerful party is in a position to impose the rules it sees as the most appropriate for the game at play.

Seeing cultures as collections of rules and metarules, rather than traits, has important implications for cross-cultural research. One of them concerns the nature of "cross-cultural" conflicts. It is suggested that cultural differences may lead to three different types of disagreement between business partners. First, they may agree on the set of rules to govern their relationship, but have divergent understandings of the content of those rules. Second, parties may disagree on how to frame their relationship ("we are friends" vs. "we are business partners"). Finally, parties may agree on the nature of their relationship and the norms governing such relationships ("we are friends who happen to do business together"), but disagree on the metarules applicable in their situation ("a friend should always be treated as a friend" vs. "business is business, even with friends"). A second point concerns the difficulty of tracing boundaries between cultures. Identity markers such as race, ethnicity, or religion traditionally used for this purpose are not always relevant for determining the cases in which specific norms are held to apply or not. For example, the favorable disposition displayed by interviewees toward other SMEs or individuals did not extend to large firms, notwithstanding the origins of their owners or employees. This uneven application of the presumption of inability could be held to signal that the norm of flexibility observed is not the expression of a Senegalese "cultural trait" so much as one deriving from the market position and level of vulnerability of SMEs. From this perspective, Senegalese SMEs might be culturally closer to foreign firms in similar situations than to the larger local firms with which they deal on a daily basis.

Trust, Cooperation, Compliance and Law

"Trust" has emerged as a major topic of interest in many lines of inquiry in recent years. However, despite widespread agreement that trust is important in a number of ways with respect to economic activity and social life in general, no widely accepted definition of the term has emerged yet. While economists consider trust as deriving from the presence of incentives to comply, the tendency in the study of cooperative relationships has been to distinguish "calculative" forms of cooperation from the more complex forms based on the emergence of "real trust". In contrast to cultural approaches, under which trust is conceptualized as a "virtue" whose origins remain unclear, economic sociologists have attempted to develop an alternative, relation-based view of the emergence of trust. From this perspective, trust is the product of an incremental process during which parties get to know each other, clarify their respective expectations, and gradually increase their levels of vulnerability, allowing them to dispense with contracts. The question then becomes one of determining the conditions required for such a process to be initiated. "Pre-existing ties" have been pointed to as important, although not essential, "priming mechanisms" for this purpose. More generally, it can be hypothesized that the initiation of business relationships requires a minimal level of confidence that the other party will behave appropriately.

Clarifying the notion of trust and how it emerges entails distinguishing between its behavioral and intentional aspects. The presence of legal or non-legal "incentives" may give rise to expectations that the other party will comply in order to avoid the application of sanctions. It does not guarantee, however, that this person will ultimately be able to comply or will refrain from taking advantage of the situation. Belief in compliance, which Sako labels "contractual trust", forms only one of three types of trust along with "competence trust" (belief in the other partys' ability to comply) and "goodwill trust" (belief in intention to cooperate) (Sako 1998, 89), the latter being based on frequent, repeated interactions giving rise to positive expectations and the formation of reciprocal attachments (Rousseau et al. 1998, 399).

Data highlight the relevance of the distinctions between, on the one hand, willingness and ability to comply, and, on the other hand, compliance and cooperation. Whereas, in Western economies, "inability" is generally used to refer to incompetence and very exceptional cases of *force majeure*, it has a much wider meaning in Dakar, where few economic actors, notwithstanding their levels of "competence", are immune from "difficulties" preventing them from satisfying their obligations. In consequence, "contractual trust" is exceptional. As to "competence trust", all one can do to assess a firm's ability to comply is to make sure that it is a *bona fide* firm and not on the verge of bankruptcy. An additional problem comes from the fact that the most able firms, i.e. those in the best competitive position, are often the ones with the least incentives to satisfy their obligations. In consequence, SMEs often have to choose between "goodwill trust" and "competence trust" when they select their partners.

The frequency of cases of inability makes it particularly important for Dakar firms to be able to distinguish real cases of inability from disguised instances of unwillingness before assigning blame for a particular problem. This is often a lengthy process requiring an assessment of the information obtained by the other party as well as other sources. A cooperative attitude, readiness to share information with the other party, and reports of problems satisfying obligations toward other parties make claims of inability more credible. However, parties facing difficulties are rarely entirely unable, and will generally manage to comply with the obligations they consider the most important for the pursuit of their activities. In such contexts, "inability" to satisfy a particular partner may in fact signal a party's unwillingness to give priority to one partner's claims over those of another. From this perspective, both unwillingness and inability are relative notions whose relevance depends on the context in which parties find themselves as well as the subjective perceptions of the individuals involved.

Data also provide interesting insights about the relationship between contractual compliance and cooperation in Dakar. In the context of industrialized economies, the question of cooperation is generally intimately connected to the notion of compliance. Although Western businesspeople do not always count on absolute, strict compliance from their partners, they nevertheless operate in a context in which they expect the major part of the vast majority of their contracts to be performed. In Stewart Macaulay's words,

> What is predictable is that contracts in the United States will be carried out in an
> acceptable fashion. When Americans make a contract, it is not certain that it will

be performed to the letter of its text or performed at all. Yet, it is a good bet that
the parties will perform acceptably (Macaulay 2003, 59).

Data indicate that, in Dakar, the contractual compliance taken for granted
in industrialized economies is neither sufficient nor necessary to establish the
presence of a cooperative frame of mind. On the one hand, Dakar SMEs tend to
interpret contractual obligations as "best efforts" ones, and are ready to contend
with breach as long as the violator acts in good faith and make efforts to minimize
the negative impact of his behavior on his partner. On the other hand, they often
expect more than strict compliance from their partners, and highly value their
capacity to behave as "real partners" and support them in times of need. It must
also be noted that the relationship between compliance and cooperation appears as
highly variable among interviewees and relationships. Whereas compliance with
contractual terms is particularly important in legal contracts, for partners it is only
one element of a larger conception of compliance encompassing all the duties
devolved upon business partners. Finally, parties to social contracts primarily seek
to comply with their social obligations: they thus give little weight to contractual
compliance and are more likely to relinquish the rights granted by law.

Data suggest that the relationship between compliance and cooperation is
not straightforward: compliance may in fact drive, or even be a prerequisite to,
future cooperative behavior, but only to the extent that it is expected from one's
partners. A brief comparison between Dakar SMEs and the Wisconsin firms
surveyed by Macaulay in 1963 illustrates this point. Although both groups of firms
are committed to solving their disputes flexibly, Wisconsin businesspeople are
supported in their endeavor by their simultaneous commitment to general norms,
holding that one has to keep one's promises and to stand behind one's products
(Macaulay 1963, 13). In other words, being flexible in Wisconsin means agreeing
to some give-and-take under the understanding that the spirit, if not the exact
letter, of the contract will be enforced. However, such norms favoring compliance,
which are congruent with the Wisconsin context, seem unlikely to emerge in the
uncertain environment prevailing in Dakar, in which the capacity to compromise
is often essential to remaining in business. While flexibility is a luxury that the
Wisconsin businessmen interviewed by Macaulay could afford, it is a basic
necessity for their Dakar counterparts.

This raises the major issue of the role played by law in the emergence of
expectations of compliance. In light of the data gathered in Dakar, it is suggested
that more consideration should be paid to the impact of observable behavior in
the generation of such expectations. Parties who frequently observe instances of
contractual breach are unlikely to hold the belief that their own contracts will be
enforced without problems. Reversing this trend would require direct action on

the root causes of contractual indiscipline, most of which, as noted above, have little to do with the legal system. This raises important doubts about the capacity of legal reform, and private law reform in particular, to generate faith in compliance in developing countries. On the positive side, however, it may de doubted that such a belief is required for markets to develop. Data show that, although the interviewees did not generally believe that their contracts would be enforced, this did not prevent them from expecting most of their partners to behave in a manner that, although distinct from compliance, was nevertheless considered acceptable. It must also be noted that the threatening (or, conversely, empowering) character of law and, consequently, its impact on expectations of compliance vary greatly among firms, relationships, and situations. Although Dakar courts represented a potential threat for most interviewees, the magnitude of this threat heavily depended on the levels of dependence between parties to a relationship, the presence of an asymmetric relationship allowing the less dependent party to dispense with law, while preventing the more dependent one to consider court use as a viable option. In consequence, increasing the reach of law in business matters may empower those players in better market positions to the potential detriment of others.

"Law and Development" or "Law and Business"? Avenues for Research

The economic turn taken on by proponents of the second law and development movement has had a major effect on its conceptualization of the issue of the "fit". In contrast to previous modernization efforts and their emphasis on the need for cultural change for development, the new movement pays lip service to the cultural roots of institutions. By defining social change in institutional terms and legal change as a matter of transition from informal to formal institutions, the movement skillfully avoids the thorny cultural issues associated with the use of legal transplants. By assuming that people choose institutions on the basis of their efficiency, it also suggests that social change through law is not only possible, but also largely unproblematic. From this perspective, the failure of reform efforts to produce the intended results necessarily derives from one of three factors: the "inefficiency" of the reforms compared to other alternatives; defects in the implementation process leading to political resistance to the new laws, despite their superiority; and the (temporary) incapacity of the local population to assess the new laws at their right value.

The major contribution of the fieldwork conducted in Dakar is to point to a more fundamental reason accounting for the marginal impact of business law reforms on business practices. It suggests that the current law and development agenda suffers from an inaccurate conceptualization of the role of law in business activity. It has been noted that, although the benchmarking initiatives of the World Bank have gone a long way to generate significant evidence of the existence of a correlation between legal institutions and economic development, the nature of the relationship between these two factors remains elusive to this day. This also applies to the issue of contract enforcement. Although state contract enforcement mechanisms are considered one of the most basic institutions required for economic development in NIE thinking, their actual relationship with levels of economic activity is far from clear. The notions that state-provided sanctions reduce the frequency of contractual breach, prevent disputes from escalating in feuds, or encourage people to deal with a wider range of partners, are more often taken for granted than clearly demonstrated, and lack the strong empirical support required for their unconditional acceptance.

The data gathered in Dakar provide good reasons to doubt that contract enforcement institutions play the central role attributed to them by law and development experts. The interviews indicate that the ways in which Dakar firms choose their contracting partners have more to do with the small size of the local market and their limited access to larger pools of partners than with their reliance on bilateral or reputation mechanisms. Similarly, the frequency of contractual violations and the high flexibility of most of the contracts entered into in Dakar do not derive from the absence of deterring sanctions as much as from the uncertainty which characterizes the local business environment. Data thus suggest that "legal insecurity" may have little to do with the actual state of legal institutions.

This finding has major policy implications. To the extent that legal institutions are only one, and often not the most important, of the many factors which influence contracting decisions and contractual compliance, achieving the "contractual security" sought after by firms and reformers would require addressing the diverse sources of uncertainty leading to high rates of breach. This would include factors such as the inadequacy of power supply and transport infrastructures, as well as the small size of the local market, which locks many firms into asymmetric relationships. In addition, among the numerous firms operating in Dakar, very few seem in the material and competitive position to privilege and impose a legal frame in their relationships and benefit from the presence of a more efficient legal system.

This not only raises doubts about the capacity of law to have an impact on business behavior in Senegal, but also provides reasons to believe that law reform can have a potentially adverse impact in developing economies. Providing more efficient legal sanctions while ignoring the real sources of contractual insecurity would not only be useless in terms of contract compliance, but would carry the risk of preventing some firms from entering into contracts, thus undermining one of the very objectives sought by legal reform in the first place. It can also be hypothesized that, by providing additional enforcement resources that only a small group of business actors are in position to use, legal reform may force less powerful players to prioritize the claims of these privileged businesses over those of other firms, and reduce the already little room to maneuver that most SMEs have to keep their businesses afloat.

Data also point to a series of measures likely to make a real difference for SMEs operating in Dakar. First, the lack of accurate information on firms present in the market limits the possibility of firms to initiate relationships and properly assess the level of risk associated with a particular transaction. The creation of reliable and well-functioning business registries and credit rating facilities would be a good step in remedying this situation. Second, the disadvantages stemming from the limited size of the local market could be limited by facilitating access to foreign markets. Measures could be taken to help Dakar firms surmount the hurdles associated with their size and the reputation of unreliability of African firms. One interviewee, e.g. mentioned that the pooling of small orders by formal associations constituted a powerful way to gain access to foreign suppliers and reduce the costs of supplies. Similarly, the establishment of close collaborative partnerships between Senegalese and foreign firms could be fostered by creating opportunities for communication and increased knowledge of the business conditions prevailing in Dakar. Finally, access to credit remains a major problem for SMEs. Microcredit facilities favored by international donors are more targeted to micro-enterprises and are clearly insufficient to solve the cash problems of SMEs and fund the investments they need in order to grow. More work would be needed in order to assess the financing needs of these firms and the reasons why such financing is not available on the Dakar market.

The present work also suggests that the failure of law and development proponents to properly assess the role of law in economic development may be traced back to their misunderstanding of the impact of law in economic activity in general. More particularly, the data cast doubts about the accuracy of the game-theory decision-making model on which the current agenda relies, and which suffers from two important limitations. First, the assumption that economic actors make decisions on the basis of the costs and benefits associated with cooperation and defection leads it to give too much weight to sanctions in general, and legal institutions, when accounting for individual behavior. Second, the emphasis put on the opportunistic nature of individuals leads to a conflation of cooperative behavior with contractual compliance, and opportunism with contractual breach. The result is a dispassionate account of the impact of law on individual behavior, which makes it possible for "expert views" of "what's best" to take precedence over local subjective perceptions of "what's not working" and "what's needed". The overemphasis put on functionality also allows for the *a priori* characterization of "informal institutions" as functional equivalents of state law, and the development of efficiency-based conceptions of the relationships between formal and informal modes of ordering.

More generally, what is at stake here is the capacity of current dominant economic and legal theories to properly account for the role of law in cooperation, as distinct from strict contractual compliance. Approaches focusing on the role of "trust" in business relationships and the "embeddedness" of economic and social relations have sought to provide additional insights into this issue. However, they have been limited by their tendency to define "law" and "trust" as opposite, mutually exclusive "modes of governance" satisfying different needs. One argument that underlies the present book is that the development of a proper understanding of the impact of the legal system on behavior requires breaking away from such dichotomies, and acknowledging that all business transactions and relationships, however "discrete" or "embedded", comprise a legal dimension as well as other aspects. Rather than looking at legal and "non legal" modes of ordering as distinct options from which transactors consciously or unconsciously choose, the emphasis should be put on the diverse ways in which they reinforce, contradict or complement each other, and on the processes by which they are accommodated by individuals.

The fieldwork conducted in Dakar represents one step in this direction. Despite the fragmentary character of the data on which it is based, the present work carries important research implications. First, it clearly reveals the lack of sophistication of approaches pointing to the existence of "informal enforcement mechanisms" developed in close-knit communities to account for the unpopularity of legal remedies in developing countries. The development of more adequate approaches to the issues of transfer failures and, more generally, legal inefficiency, would require the clarification of the respective roles of law, culture, social structure, and bargaining power in the management of business relationships in developing and industrialized economies.

This book provides fruitful avenues for further exploration of these questions. A first one would consist in abandoning categorizations of relationships based on external variables (e.g. strength of relationship, network structure, personal similaritie …) that determine the role played by law in them. Data suggest that the role ascribed to law in specific situations might be better understood by considering the "frames" used by the parties to define their relationship and the problem they face. As mentioned before, data indicate that the business contracts entered into in Dakar are framed in three main ways. In "legal contracts", which are those closer to the promise-based conceptions prevailing in legal theory, legal sanctions are used to ensure compliance as well as signal willingness to strictly enforce contracts.

In contrast, recourse to law is almost excluded in social contracts, which rely essentially on social pressure, and give priority to the informal norms governing the relationships over the enforcement of the promises made. Partnership contracts for their part rely primarily on bilateral mechanisms aiming at cooperative behavior not limited to, nor necessarily congruent with, strict compliance. Data also indicate that the "frame" that will be applied to a relationship is influenced by a variety of factors, including personal values and preferences and the nature and strength of the ties between the parties and within the network in which the relationship is inscribed, but is not the product of any or all of these factors. Framing is better seen as an active process influenced by strategic considerations, as shown by the diverse strategies mentioned by interviewees to favor or limit the application of a certain "frame" to a specific relationship. In addition, since the framing process lasts as long as the parties keep interacting with each other, the "frame" governing a relation is not set once and for all from the start, but evolves in the course of the relationship. It is argued that focusing on the framing process would allow for a better understanding of the nature of trust, the processes through which it emerges, and its impact in specific situations.

A second avenue for research concerns the investigation of the impact of culture on business behavior. The difficulty of clearly defining the boundaries of the communities relevant for the analysis of the situation of Dakar SMEs suggests that cultural identity is ultimately a matter of self-perception and identification with particular groups of people, rather than the product of specific factors. Cultural identification is made on the basis of subjective criteria, the elements distinguishing "in-group" from "out-group" members often remaining implicit or even unconscious. A better understanding of this process could provide major insights into the factors that may account for behavior generally attributed to the existence of culturally inherited traits. For example, interviewees were more inclined to be flexible in their dealings with firms in similar positions than with larger ones, suggesting that contractual flexibility may not be the expression of cultural values of solidarity and compromise as much as the product of the "fundamental attribution error", which leads people to ascribe their own failures (and those of members of their groups) to adverse circumstances and blame those of outsiders on their personality.

A final interesting avenue for research concerns the evolution of business practices in Dakar in the context of globalization, and its potential impact on economic development. Although more data would be needed to show the existence of a trend, many younger interviewees had acquired some professional training in business management, and/or had lived in Europe or North America, and seemed more inclined than their older counterparts to adopt the business models dominant in those parts of the world. Direct exposure to such ways of doing business while working for or with large local firms or foreign organizations also seemed to provide interviewees with models they attempted to apply, with some adaptations, in their own business. An important question concerns the potential impact of such transformations of Dakar's society on the role played by law in contract enforcement. On the one hand, greater exposure to foreign models may lead to an increased professionalization of firms and a clearer separation between business and personal considerations, leading to a gradual shift from "social" to other types of relationships. As Idrissa says,

> There is a huge difference between people from my generation and younger people; I lived through the last years of colonization, I left Senegal for the first time when I was 24, whereas my son left before he was 20, first for France, and now in the US. He's more of a North Americano-European than an African by now. When he's back, he will not have the same values as I do, for sure, he won't follow the same rule ...

Yet, even though more stringent business standards might eventually render some instances of excusable breach less excusable and thus reduce the level of flexibility displayed by firms, the adaptive nature of such flexibility in the context in which Dakar firms operate suggests that it is unlikely to lose its appeal in the near future. A general movement from "partnership" forms of cooperation toward more legal forms can hardly be foreseen, notwithstanding the amount of effort spent on improving Dakar's investment climate.

Appendix A

The following table provides information on the participants to the study and the firms they represent. The number of employees refers includes full-time permanent and temporary employees and reflects seasonal variations where relevant.

Pseudonym	Firm creation	Industry	Number of employees
Abdou	1982	Sales – automotive	33
Abdoulaye	2000	Sales and consulting services – information technology	5
Aicha	2004	Manufacturing – plastic products	20
Alassane	1988 (from split up)	Sales – automotive	60–100
Aliou	Formalized in 1990	Trade and manufacturing – clothing	25
Almamy	2005	Manufacturing – food	16–40
Amir	1980	Industry – plastic products	150–250
Babacar	1991	Manufacturing – clothing	30
Bassirou	1974	Sales – food	8
Cheik	2000	Sales and maintenance services – information technology	5
Cherif	1990	Construction	7
Djibril	1985	Sales – textile	40
Eric	2002	Sales and maintenance services – appliances	10
Ibrahima	1994	Manufacturing – metal products	27
Idrissa	1992	Consulting services	5
Issa	1991	Manufacturing – building materials	10–30
Jacques	2001	Sales – office supplies	23
Lamine	1999	Sales – clothing	9
Mansour	1980	Manufacturing – chemicals	90
Moktar	2004	Construction	10
Moussa	Formalized in 2003	Sales – food	50
Moustapha	1998	Education	7
Pape	2000	Construction	9–40

Pseudonym	Firm creation	Industry	Number of employees
Pierre	2003	Education	7
Robert	1993 (from split up)	Sales and maintenance services – building materials	13–40
Saliou	2001	Sales and maintenance services – medical supplies	8
Serigne	1993	Manufacturing – chemicals	70–100
Seydou	1975	Manufacturing – building materials	64
Thierno	1962	Manufacturing – furniture	20–100
Yacine	1972	Sales – clothing	10

Bibliography

La connaissance du droit en Afrique. Actes du symposium, Bruxelles, 2-3 décembre 1983 (1984, Bruxelles: Académie Royale des sciences d'outre-mer).

La rédaction des coutumes dans le passé et dans le présent: colloque des 16-17 mai 1960 (1962, Bruxelles: Éditions de l'Institut de sociologie).

L'harmonisation du droit des affaires en Afrique. Actes du colloque, Rome, 4-6 décembre 1972 (1974, Milan: Guiffré).

'Notes and News: Progress in African Legal Studies', (1959) *Journal of African Law* 3: 145–51.

The Future of Customary Law in Africa – L'avenir du droit coutumier en Afrique. Symposium-colloque, Amsterdam, 1955 (1956, Leiden: Universitaire Pers Leiden).

Abarchi, D. (2000), 'La supranationalité de l'Organisation pour l'Harmonisation en Afrique du Droit des Affaires (OHADA)', *Revue burkinabè de droit* 37: 9–27.

Abarchi, D. (2003), 'Problématique des réformes législatives en Afrique: le mimétisme juridique comme méthode de construction du Droit', *Recueil Penant* 113: 842, 88–105.

Abel, R.L. (1979), 'Western Courts in Non-Western settings: Patterns of Court Use in Colonial and Neo-Colonial Africa', in *The Imposition of Law* (ed.) S.B. Burman and B.E. Harrell-Bond (New York: Academic Press), 167–200.

Acheson, J.A. (1990), 'The Social Organization of the Maine Lobster Market', in *Markets and Marketing* (ed.) S. Plattner (Lanham, MD: University Press of the Americas), 105–30.

Adelman, S. and Paliwala, A. (1993), *Law and Development in Crisis* (London: Hans Zell).

Adido, R. (2002), *Essai sur l'application du droit en Afrique: le cas de l'O.H.A.D.A. Aspects sociologiques et juridiques au vu du passé et du présent* (Villeneuve d'Ascq: Presses universitaires du septentrion).

Adotévi, A. (1998), 'Les lacunes du nouveau droit des affaires harmonisé', *Jeune Afrique Économie* 1–14 June 1998, 136.

Akerloff, G. (1970), 'The Market of "Lemons": Quality Uncertainty and the Market Mechanism', *Quarterly Journal of Economics* 84, 488–500.

Alibert, J. (1990), 'Justice et développement économique: le point de vue des entreprises', *Afrique contemporaine* 156, 72–82.

Alibert, J. (1999), 'Le centre d'arbitrage, de médiation et de conciliation de la Chambre de commerce de la Région de Dakar', *Marchés tropicaux et méditerranéens* 21 may 1999, 1035–9.

Alliot, M. (1965), 'Les résistances traditionnelles au droit moderne dans les États d'Afrique francophones et à Madagascar', in *Études de droit africain et de droit malgache* (ed.) J. Poirier (Paris: Cujas), 235–56.

Allott, A. (1960a), *Essays in African Law: With Special Reference to the Law of Ghana* (London: Butterworth).

Allott, A. (ed.) (1960b), *The Future of Law in Africa. Record of Proceedings of the London Conference, 28 December 1959 – 8 January 1960* (London: Butterworth).

Allott, A. (1963), 'Legal Development and Economic Growth in Africa', in *Changing Law in Developing Countries* (ed.) J.N.D. Anderson (London: George Allen & Unwin), 194–209.

Allott, A. (1965a), 'La place des coutumes juridiques africaines dans les systèmes juridiques africains modernes', in *Études de droit africain et de droit malgache* (ed.) J. Poirier (Paris: Cujas), 257–66.

Allott, A. (1965b), *The Future of Law in Africa* (Berkeley: University of California Press).

Allott, A. (1970), *New Essays in African Law* (London: Butterworth).

Allott, A. (1975), 'Credit and the Law in Africa: a Special Study of Some Legal Aspects of Economic Development', *Journal of African Law* 19, 73–83.

Allott, A. (1980), *L'influence du droit anglais sur les systèmes juridiques africains* (Paris: Economica).

Allott, A. (1984), *On Knowledge of Customary Laws in Africa* (Bruxelles: Académie Royale des sciences d'outre-mer).

Amin, S. (1976), *Impérialisme et sous-développement en Afrique* (Paris: Anthropos).

Amselle, J.-L. (1971), *Parenté et commerce chez les Kooroko* (London: Oxford University Press for the International African Institute).

Amselle, J.-L. (1977), *Les négociants de la savane* (Paris: Anthropos).

Arboussier, G.d'. (1963), 'L'évolution de la législation dans les pays africains d'expression française et à Madagascar', in *African Law: Adaptation and Development* (ed). H. Kuper and L. Kuper (Los Angeles: University of California Press), 165–83.

Argyres, N.S., Bercovitz, J. and Mayer, K.J. (2007), 'Complementarity and Evolution of Contractual Provisions: An Empirical Study of IT Services Contracts', *Organization Science* 18, 3–19.

Asozou, A.A. (2001), *International Commercial Arbitration and African States* (Cambridge: Cambridge University Press).

Assi-Esso, A.-M.H. and Diouf, N. (2002), *OHADA – Recouvrement des créances* (Bruxelles: Bruylant).

Association Henri Capitant des amis de la culture juridique française (2006), *Les droits civilistes en question. A propos des rapports Doing Business de la Banque mondiale* (Paris: Société de législation comparée).

Aviram, A. (2004), 'A Paradox of Spontaneous Formation: The Evolution of Private Legal Systems', *Yale Law and Policy Review* 22, 1–68.

Ba, S. (2003), 'Rapport d'activités de la Cour commune de justice et d'arbitrage de l'OHADA (CCJA) – Année 2002', *Journal Officiel de l'OHADA* 13, 28–33.

Baker, W.E. (1990), 'Market Networks and Corporate Behavior', *American Journal of Sociology* 96, 589–625.

Barry, B. and Harding, L. (eds) (1992), *Commerce et commerçants en Afrique de l'Ouest: le Sénégal* (Paris: L'Harmattan).

Batenburg, R.S., Raub, W. and Snidjers, C. (2003), 'Contacts and Contracts: Dyadic Embeddedness and the Contractual Behavior of Firms', in *The Governance of Relations in Markets and Organizations* (eds) V. Buskens, W. Raub and C. Snijders (Oxford: JAI/Elsevier), 135–88.

Baumann, E. (1998), '"Chez nous, c'est 10% par mois!" Coût du crédit et représentation du temps en milieu populaire à Dakar', in *Les opérateurs économiques et l'État au Sénégal* (eds) L. Harding, L. Marfaing and M. Sow (Hamburg: LIT), 189–202.

Beale, H. and Dugdale, T. (1975), 'Contracts between Businessmen: Planning and the Use of Contractual Remedies', *British Journal of Law and Society* 2, 45–60.

Beauchard, R. and Koko, M.J.V. (2011), 'Can OHADA Increase Legal Certainty in Africa?' *Justice and Development Working Paper* no 17/2011.

Beckert, J. (1996), 'What is Sociological about Economic Sociology? Uncertainty and the Embeddedness of Economic Action', *Theory and Society* 25, 806–40.

Beckert, J. (2003), 'Economic Sociology and Embeddedness: How Shall We Conceptualize Economic Action?' *Journal of Economic Issues* 37, 769–87.

Beckstrom, J.H. (1973), 'Transplantation of Legal Systems: An Early Report on the Reception of Western Laws in Ethiopia', *American Journal of Comparative Law* 21, 557–83.

Benda-Beckmann, F. (1989), 'Scapegoat and Magic Charm: Law in Development Theory and Practice', *Journal of Legal Pluralism* 28, 129–48.

Benda-Beckman, F. (2003), 'Mysteries of Capital or Mystification of Legal Property?' *FOCAAL-European Journal of Anthropology* 41, 187–91.

Benkemoun, L. (2003), 'Quelques réflexions sur l'OHADA, 10 ans après le traité de Port-Louis', *Penant: revue de droit des pays d'Afrique* 113, 133–9.

Benton, L. (1996), 'From the World Systems Perspective to Institutional World History: Culture and Economy in Global Theory', *Journal of World History* 7:2, 261–95.

Benton, L. (2002), *Law and Colonial Cultures: Legal Regimes in World History* (Cambridge: Cambridge University Press).

Berkowitz, D., Pistor, K. and Richard, J.-F. (2003a), 'Economic Development, Legality and the Transplant Effect', *European Economic Review* 47:1, 165–95.

Berkowitz, D., Pistor, K. and Richard, J.-F. (2003b), 'The Transplant Effect', *American Journal of Comparative Law* 51:1, 163–204.

Bernstein, E.E. (1995), 'Law & Economics and the Structure of Value Adding Contracts: A Contract Lawyer's View of the Law & Economics Literature', *Oregon Law Review* 74, 189–238.

Bernstein, L. (1992), 'Opting Out of the Legal System: Extralegal Contracting in the Diamond Industry', *Journal of Legal Studies* 21, 115–57.

Bernstein, L. (1995), 'The Silicon Valley Lawyer as Transaction Cost Engineer?' *Oregon Law Review* 74, 239–56.

Bernstein, L. (1996), 'Merchant Law in a Merchant Court: Rethinking the Code's Search for Immanent Business Norms', *University of Pennsylvania Law Review* 144, 1765–1821.

Bernstein, L. (1999), 'The Questionable Empirical Basis of Article 2's Incorporation Strategy: A Preliminary Study', *University of Chicago Law Review* 66, 710–80.

Bernstein, L. (2001), 'Private Commercial Law in the Cotton Industry: Creating Cooperation through Rules, Norms, and Institutions', *Michigan Law Review* 99, 1724–90.

Betts, R.F. (1970), *Association and Assimilation in French Colonial Theory, 1890-1914* (New York: AMS Press).

Bierbrauer, G. (1994), 'Toward an Understanding of Legal Culture: Variations in Individualism and Collectivism between Kurds, Lebanese, and Germans', *Law and Society Review* 28, 243–64.

Biggart, N.W. and Beaemish, T.D. (2003), 'The Economic Sociology of Conventions: Habit, Custom, Practice, and Routine in Market Order', *Annual Review of Sociology* 29, 443–64.

Bigsten, A., Collier, P., Dercon, S., Fafchamps, M., Gauthier, B., Gunning, J.W., Oduro, A., Oostendorp, R., Patillo, C., Soderbom, M., Teal, F. and Zeufack, A. (2000), 'Contract Flexibility and Dispute Resolution in African Manufacturing', *Journal of Development Studies* 36:4, 1–37.

Blanc-Jouvan, X. (1977), 'La résistance du droit africain à la modernisation', *Revue sénégalaise de droit* 21, 21–44.

Blankenburg, E. (1994), 'The Infrastructure for Avoiding Civil Litigation: Comparing Cultures of Legal Behavior in the Netherlands and West Germany', *Law and Society Review* 28, 789–808.

Blumberg, B.F. (2001), 'Cooperation Contracts between Embedded Firms', *Organization Studies* 22, 825–52.

Bohannan, P. (1955), 'Some Principles of Exchange and Investment Among the Tiv', *American Anthropologist* 57, 60–70.

Bruno, M. and Pleskovic, B. (ed.) (1996), *Annual World Bank Conference on Development Economics* (Washington, D.C.: World Bank).

Burg, E.M. (1977), 'Law and Development: A review of the Literature and a Critique of "Scholars in Self-Estrangement"', *American Journal of Comparative Law* 25, 492–530.

Burt, R.S. (2001), 'Bandwidth and Echo: Trust, Information, and Gossip in Social Networks', in *Networks and Markets* (eds) J.E. Rauch and A. Casella (New York: Russell Sage), 30–74.

Buskens, V. (2002), *Social Networks and Trust* (Boston: Kluwer).

Cao, L. (1997), 'Law and Economic Development: A New Beginning?' *Texas International Law Journal* 32, 545–59.

Cao, L. (2004), 'The Ethnic Question in Law and Development', *Michigan Law Review* 102, 1044–1103.

Carothers, T. (2006), 'The Problem of Knowledge', in *Promoting the Rule of Law Abroad: In Seach of Knowledge* (ed.) T. Carothers (Washington, DC: Carnegie Endowment For International Peace), 15–28.

Carty, A. (ed.) (1992), *Law and Development* (New York: New York University Press).

Chabas, J. (1962), 'Transformation du droit local et évolution économique', *Annales africaines* 151–9.

Chabas, J. (1965), 'La réforme judiciaire et le droit coutumier dans les États africains qui formaient les anciennes fédérations de l'A.O.F. et de l'A.E.F.', in *Études de droit africain et de droit malgache* (ed.) J. Poirier (Paris: Cujas), 267–79.

Chanock, M. (1985), *Law, Custom and Social Order* (Cambridge: Cambridge University Press).

Chanock, M. (1992), 'The Law Market: The Legal Encounter in British East and Central Africa', in *European Expansion and the Law* (eds) W.J. Mommsen and J.A. De Moor (Oxford: Berg), 279–305.

Chanock, M. (1995), 'Neither Customary nor Legal: African Customary Law in an Era of Family Law Reform', in *African Law and Legal Theory* (eds) G.R. Woodman and A.O. Obilade (New York: New York University Press), 171–90.

Charny, D. (1990), 'Non Legal Sanctions in Commercial Relationships', *Harvard Law Review* 104, 373–467.

Chibundu, M.O. (1997), 'Law in Development: On Tapping, Gourding and Serving Palm-Wine', *Case Western Reserve Journal of International Law* 29, 167–262.

Chua, A. (1998), 'Markets, Democracy and Ethnicity: Toward a New Paradigm for Law and Development', *Yale Law Journal* 108, 1–107.

Chua, A. (2000), 'The Paradox of Free Market Democracy: Rethinking Development Policy', *Harvard International Law Journal* 41, 287–379.

Clague, C. (1997), *Institutions and Development, Growth, and Governance in Less-Developed and Post-Socialist Countries* (Baltimore, MD: John Hopkins University Press).

Claro, D.P., Hagelaar, G. and Omta, O. (2003), 'The Determinants of Relational Governance and Performance: How to Manage Business Relationships?' *Industrial Marketing Management* 32, 703–16.

Clay, K. (1997), 'Trade Without Law: Private-Order Institutions in Mexican California', *The Journal of Law, Economics, & Organization* 13, 202–31.

Coase, R. (1937), 'The Nature of the Firm', *Economica* 4, 385–405.

Cohen, A. (1971), *Cultural Strategies in the Organization of Trading Diasporas* (London: Oxford University Press for the International African Institute).

Collins, H. (1999), *Regulating Contracts* (Oxford: Oxford University Press).

Commissions nationales OHADA (2011), *Rapport de la réunion plénière des commissions nationales OHADA*. Bamako, 12-14 July 2011.

Conac, G. (1980), *La vie du droit en Afrique* (Paris: Economica).

Cooter, R. (2007–2008), 'Doing What You Say: Contracts and Economic Development', *Alabama Law Review* 59, 1107–33.

Cooter, R. and Landa, J.T. (1984), 'Personal Versus Impersonal Trade: The Size of Trading Groups and Contract Law', *International Review of Law and Economics* 4, 15–22.

Copans, J. (2000), 'Mourides des champs, Mourides des villes, Mourides du téléphone portable et de l'Internet – les renouvellements de l'économie politique d'une confrérie', *Afrique contemporaine* 194, 24–33.

Cowen, M. and Shenton, R. (1995), 'The Invention of Development', in *Power of Development* (ed.) J. Crush (London: Routledge), 27–43.

Crowder, M. (1968), *West Africa Under Colonial Rule* (London: Hutchinson).

Curtin, P.D. (1971), *Imperialism* (New York: Walker).

Dalmeida Mele, F. (2010), 'Tendances jurisprudentielles de la CCJA par pays de provenance du pourvoi', *Revue de Droit Uniforme Africain* 3, 58–61.

Daniels, R.J. and Trebilcock, M.J. (2004), 'The Political Economy of Rule of Law Reform in Developing Countries', *Michigan Journal of International Law* 26, 99–140.

Darby, P. (1987), *Three Faces of Imperialism: British and American Approaches to Asia and Africa 1870-1970* (New Haven: Yale University Press).

Dareste, P. (1931), *Traité de droit colonial*, tome 2, vol. 2 (Paris).

Darian-Smith, E. and Fitzpatrick, P. (eds) (1999), *Laws of the Postcolonial* (Ann Arbor: University of Michigan Press).

Darr, A. (2003), 'Gifting Practices and Interorganizational Relations: Constructing Obligation Networks in the Electronics Sector', *Sociological Forum* 18, 31–51.

Darr, A. (2007), 'The Mutual Weaving of Obligation Networks in Mass Industrial Markets', *Current Sociology* 55, 41–58.

Date-Bah, S.K. (1973), 'Aspects of the Role of Contract in the Economic Development of Ghana', *Journal of African Law* 17, 254–70.

David, R. (1962), 'La refonte du Code civil dans les États africains', *Annales africaines* 160–70.

David, R. (1963), 'A Civil Code for Ethopia: Considerations on the Codification of the Civil Law in African Countries', *Tulane Law Review* 37, 187.

David, R. and Jauffret-Spinosi, C. (1988), *Les grands systèmes de droit contemporains*, 9th ed. (Paris: Dalloz).

Davidson, B. (1978), *Let Freedom Come: Africa in Modern History*, 1st American ed. (Boston: Little, Brown and Company).

Davis, K.E. (2001), 'The Rules of Capitalism', *Third World Quarterly* 22, 675–82.

Davis, K.E. (2004), 'What Can the Rule of Law Variable Tell us About Rule of Law Reforms?' *Michigan Journal of International Law* 26, 141–61.

Davis, K.E. and Trebilcock, M.J. (2001), 'Legal Reforms and Development', *Third World Quarterly* 22, 21–36.

Davis, K.E. and Trebilcock, M.J. (2008), 'The Relationship between Law and Development: Optimists versus Skeptics', *American Journal of Comparative Law* 56, 895–946.

Davis, K., Trebilcock, M.J. and Heys, B. (2001), 'Ethnically Homogeneous Commercial Elites in Developing Countries', *Law & Policy in International Business* 32, 331–361.

de Mesquita, E.B. and Stephenson, M. (2003), 'Legal Institutions and the Structure of Informal Networks', *Harvard Law and Economics Discussion Paper* no 419.

De Saussure, L. (1899), *La psychologie de la colonisation française dans ses rapports avec les sociétés indigènes* (Paris: Félix Alcan).

de Soto, H. (1989), *The Other Path: The Invisible Revolution in the Third World* (New York: Harper & Row).

de Soto, H. (2000), *The Mystery of Capital* (New York: Basic Books).

Deakin, S., Lane, C. and Wilkinson, F. (1994), '"Trust" or Law? Toward an Integrated Theory of Contractual Relations between Firms', *Journal of Law and Society* 21, 329–49.

Decottignies, R. (1962), 'Réflexions sur le projet de code sénégalais des obligations', *Annales africaines* 171–80.

Decottignies, R. (1964), 'L'apport européen dans l'élaboration du droit privé sénégalais', *Annales africaines* 79–113.

Decottignies, R. (1977), 'La résistance du droit africain à la modernisation en matière d'obligations', *Revue sénégalaise de droit* 21, 59–78.

Deschamps, H. (1953), *Les méthodes et les doctrines coloniales de la France du XVIe siècle à nos jours* (Paris: A. Colin).

Deschamps, H. (1963), 'Et maintenant Lord Lugard?' *Africa* 33, 296–306.

Dezalay, Y. and Garth, B. (1997), 'Law, Lawyers and Social Capital: "Rule of Law" versus Relational Capitalism', *Social and Legal Studies*, 6:1, 109–41.

Dia, M. (1991), 'Development and Cultural Values in Sub-Saharan Africa', *Finance and Development* 28, 10–13.

Dia, M. (1996), *Africa's Management in the 1990s and Beyond: Reconciling Indigenous and Transplanted Institutions* (Washington, D.C.: The World Bank).

Dickerson, C.M. (2005), 'Harmonizing Business Laws in Africa: OHADA Calls the Tune', *Columbia Journal of Transnational Law* 44:1, 17–73.

DiMaggio, P. (1994), 'Culture and Economy', in *The Handbook of Economic Sociology* (eds) N. Smesler and R. Swedberg (Princeton: Princeton University Press), 27–57.

DiMaggio, P. and Lough, H. (1998), 'Socially Embedded Consumer Transactions: For What Kinds of Purchases Do People Most Often Use Networks?' *American Sociological Review* 63, 619–37.

Dimier, V. (2002), 'Direct or Indirect Rule: Propaganda Around a Scientific Controversy', in *Promoting the Colonial Idea: Propaganda and Visions of Empire in France* (eds) T. Chafer and A. Sackur (London: Palgrave (Macmillan)), 168–83.

Dimier, V. (2004), *Le gouvernement des colonies: regards croisés franco-britanniques* (Bruxelles: Éditions de l'Université de Bruxelles).

Diop, M.C. (2002), *Le Sénégal contemporain* (Paris: Karthala).

Diop, M.-C. (ed.) (2002), *La société sénégalaise entre le local et le global* (Paris: Karthala).

Diop, M.-C. and Diouf, M. (1999), 'Sénégal: par-delà la succession Senghor-Diouf', in *Les figures du politique en Afrique. Des pouvoirs hérités aux pouvoirs élus* (eds) M.C. Diop and M. Diouf (Paris: Karthala), 139–88.

Diouf, I. (2003), *Le secteur informel au Sénégal de l'indépendance à nos jours: concepts, caractéristiques, facteurs de progression et perspectives* (Dakar: Goethe Institut Inter Nationes).

Diouf, M. (2000), 'Assimilation coloniale et identités religieuses de la civilité des originaires des Quatre communes (Sénégal)', *Canadian Journal of African Studies* 34, 565–87.

Diouf, M. (2001), *Histoire du Sénégal: le modèle islamo-wolof et ses périphéries* (Paris: Maisonneuve & Larose).

Dislère, P. (1914), *Traité de législation coloniale*, 4th edition (Paris: Dupont).

Douglas, M. (2004), 'Traditional Culture – Let's Hear No More About It', in *Culture and Public Action* (eds) V. Rao and M. Walton (Stanford, CA: Stanford University Press), 85–109.

Dozon, J.-P. (2003), *Frères et sujets: La France et l'Afrique en perspective* (Paris: Flammarion).

Dulsrud, A. and Gronhaug, K. (2007), 'Is Friendship Consistent With Competitive Market Exchange? A Microsociological Analysis of the Fish Export-Import Business', *Acta Sociologica* 50, 7–19.

Dyer, J.H. and Singh, H. (1998), 'The Relational View: Cooperative Strategy and Sources of Interorganizational Competitive Advantage', *Academy of Management Review* 23, 660–79.

Edwards, J. and Ogilvie, S. (2011), 'Contract Enforcement, Institutions, and Social Capital: The Maghribi Traders Reappraised', *The Economic History Review* doi: 10.1111/j.1468-0289.2011.00635.x.

Elias, T.O. (1954), 'Customary Law: The Limits of its Validity in Colonial Law', *African Studies* 13:3–4, 97–107.

Elias, T.O. (1962), *British Colonial Law: A Comparative Study of the Interaction Between English and Local Laws in British Dependencies* (London: Stevens & Sons).

Elias, T.O. (1965), *The Evolution of Law and Government in Modern Africa* (Berkeley: University of California Press).

Ellickson, R.C. (1991), *Order Without Law: How Neighbors Settle Disputes* (Cambridge, MA: Harvard University Press).

Ellickson, R.C. (1998), 'Law and Economics Discovers Social Norms', *The Journal of Legal Studies* 27, 537–52.

Esser, J.P. (1996), 'Institutionalizing Industry: The Changing Forms of Contract', *Law and Social Inquiry* 21, 593–629.

Esteva, G. (1992), 'Development', in *The Development Dictionary: A Guide to Knowledge as Power* (ed.) W. Sachs (London: Zed Books), 6–25.

Etounga Manguellé, D. (1991), *L'Afrique a-t-elle besoin d'un programme d'ajustement culturel?* (Paris: Nouvelles du Sud).

Fafchamps, M. (1996), 'The Enforcement of Commercial Contracts in Ghana', *World Development* 24, 427–48.

Fafchamps, M. (2000), 'Ethnicity and Credit in Trade Manufacturing', *Journal of Development Economics* 61, 205–35.

Fafchamps, M. (2001a), 'Networks, Communities and Markets in Sub-Saharan Africa: Implications for Firm Growth and Investment', *Journal of African Economies* 10 suppl., 109–42.

Fafchamps, M. (2001b), 'The Role of Business Networks in Market Development in Sub-Saharan Africa', in *Communities and Markets in Economic Development* (eds) M. Aoki and Y. Hayami (Oxford: Oxford University Press), 186–214.

Fafchamps, M. (2002), 'Spontaneous Market Emergence', *The B.E. Journal of Theoretical Economics* 2:1, Article 2. Available at: http://www.bepress.com/bejte/topics/vol2/iss1/art2.

Fafchamps, M. (2004), *Market Institutions in Sub-Saharan Africa* (Cambridge, MA: The MIT Press).

Fafchamps, M. and Minten, B. (1999), 'Relationships and Traders in Madagascar', *Journal of Development Studies* 35:6, 1–35.

Fafchamps, M. and Minten, B. (2001), 'Property Rights in a Flea Market Economy', *Economic Development and Cultural Change* 49, 229–67.

Fanselow, F.S. (1990), 'The Bazaar Economy or How Bizarre is the Bazaar Really?' *Man* 25:2, 250–65.

Farnsworth, E.A. (1964), 'Law Reform in a Developing Country: a New Code of Obligations for Senegal', *Journal of African Law* 8, 6–19.

Faundez, J. (ed.) (1997), *Good Government and the Law* (New York: St.Martin's Press).

Feinman, J.M. (2000), 'Relational Contract Theory in Context', *Northwestern University Law Review* 94, 737–48.

Feldman, E.A. (2006), 'The Tuna Court: Law and Norms in the World's Premier Fish Market', *California Law Review* 94, 313–69.

Feldman, E.A. (2007), 'Law, Culture, and Conflict: Dispute Resolution in Postwar Japan', in *Law in Japan: A Turning Point?* (ed.) D.H. Foote (Seattle: University of Washington Press), 50–79.

Felstiner, W.L.F., Abel, R.L. and Sarat, A. (1980), ,The Emergence and Transformation of Disputes: Naming, Blaming, Claiming...', *Law and Society Review* 15, 631–54.

Fitzpatrick, P. (1993), 'Law's Infamy', in *Law and Development in Crisis* (eds) S. Adelman and A. Paliwala (London: Hans Zell), 27–50.

Forneris, X. (2001), 'Harmonising Commercial Law in Africa: the OHADA', *Juris Périodique* 46, 77–85.

Fouchard, P. (ed.) (2000), *L'OHADA et les perspectives de l'arbitrage en Afrique. Actes du premier colloque du Centre René-Jean Dupuy pour le droit et le développement, Yaoundé, 13-14 décembre 1999* (Bruxelles: Bruylant).

Friedman, L.M. (1969), 'On Legal Development', *Rutgers Law Review* 24, 11–64.

Friedman, L.M. (1975), *The Legal System: A Social Science Perspective* (New York: Russell Sage Foundation).

Frilet, M. (2001), 'L'OHADA ou l'harmonisation du droit des affaires en Afrique: Une expérience unique et une réalité prometteuse', *International Law FORUM du droit international* 3, 163–71.

Fukuyama, F. (1995), *Trust: The Social Virtues and the Creation of Prosperity* (New York: Free Press).

Fukuyama, F. (2001), 'Social Capital, Civil Society and Development', *Third World Quarterly* 22:1, 7–20.

Garth, B.G. (2003), 'Law and Society as Law and Development', *Law and Society Review* 37, 305–14.

Geertz, C. (1963), *Peddlers and Princes: Social Change and Economic Modernization in Two Indonesian Towns* (Chicago: University of Chicago Press).

Geertz, C. (1978), 'The Bazaar Economy: Information and Search in Peasant Marketing', *American Economic Review* 68:2, 28–32.

Geertz, C. (1983), *Local Knowledge: Further Essays in Interpretive Anthropology* (New York: Basic Books).

Gendarme, R. (1966), 'Problèmes juridiques et développement économique', in *Les aspects juridiques du développement économique – Legal Aspects of Economic Development* (ed.) A. Tunc (Paris: Dalloz), 25–58.

Ghai, Y. (1987), 'Law, Development and African Scholarship', *Modern Law Review* 50, 750–76.

Ghai, Y. (1969), *Customary Contracts and Transactions in Kenya* (London: Oxford University Press).

Ginsburg, T. (2000), 'Does Law Matter for Economic Development? Evidence From East Asia', *Law and Society Review* 34, 829–46.

Girault, A. (1943), *Principes de colonisation et de législation coloniale*, 6th ed. (Paris: Sirey).

Gluckman, M. (1966), 'Legal Aspects of Development in Africa: Problems and Research Arising from the Study of Traditional Systems of Law', in *Les aspects juridiques du développement économique – Legal Aspects of Economic Development* (ed.) A. Tunc (Paris: Dalloz), 59–74.

Gómez, M.A. (2008), 'All in the Family: The Influence of Social Networks on Dispute Processing (A Case Study of a Developing Economy)', *Georgia Journal of International Law* 36, 291–353.

Gonidec, P.-F. (1976), *Les droits africains: Évolution et sources*, 2nd ed. (Paris: Librairie générale de droit et de jurisprudence).

Gordon, R.W. (1985), 'Macaulay, Macneil, and the Discovery of Solidarity and Power in Contract Law', *Wisconsin Law Review* 565–580.

Granovetter, M. (1985), 'Economic Action and Social Structure: The Problem of Embeddedness', *American Journal of Sociology* 91, 481–510.

Granovetter, M. (1995), 'The Economic Sociology of Firms and Entrepreneurs', in *The Economic Sociology of Immigration: Essays on Networks, Ethnicity and Entrepreneurship* (ed.) A. Portes (New York: Russell Sage Foundation), 128–65.

Granovetter, M. (2002), 'A Theoretical Agenda for Economic Sociology', in *The New Economic Sociology: Developments in an Emerging Field* (eds) M. F. Guillén, R. Collins, P. England and M. Meyer (New York: Russell Sage Foundation), 35–60.

Greif, A. (1989), 'Reputation and Coalitions in Medieval Trade: Evidence on the Maghribi Traders', *Journal of Economic History* 49:4, 857–82.

Greif, A. (1993), 'Contract Enforceability and Economic Institutions in Early Trade: The Maghribi Traders' Coalition', *American Economic Review* 83, 525–48.

Greif, A. (1994), 'Cultural Beliefs and the Organization of Society: A Historical and Theoretical Reflection on Collectivist and Individualist Societies', *The Journal of Political Economy* 102, 912–50.

Gueye, B. (2002), 'Les transformations de l'État en Afrique: l'exemple du Sénégal', *Revue internationale de droit africain, Revue EDJA* 54, 7–50.

Guiso, L., Sapienza, P. and Zingales, L. (2004), 'The Role of Social Capital in Financial Development', *The American Economic Review* 94, 526–56.

Hadfield, G. (2000), 'Privatizing Commercial Law: Lessons from the Middle and Digital Ages', *John M. Olin Program in Law & Economics Working Paper* no 195.

Hadfield, G. (2005), 'The Many Legal Institutions That Support Contractual Commitments', in *Handbook of New Institutional Economics* (eds) C. Menard and M.M. Shirley (Dordrecht: Springer), 175–203.

Hailey, L. (1957), *An African Survey Revised 1956* (London: Oxford University Press).

Haley, J.O. (1978), 'The Myth of the Reluctant Litigant', *Journal of Japanese Studies* 4, 359–90.

Harding, L., Marfaing, L. and Sow, M. (eds) (1998), *Les opérateurs économiques et l'État au Sénégal* (Hamburg: LIT).

Harmand, J. (1910), *Domination et colonisation* (Paris: Flammarion).

Harrison, L.E. (2000a), *Underdevelopment is a State of Mind: The Latin American Case* (Lanham: Madison Books).

Harrison, L.E. (2000b), 'Why Culture Matters', in *Culture Matters: How Values Shape Human Progress* (eds) L.E. Harrison and S.P. Huntington (New York: Basic Books), xvii–xxxiv.

Harrison, L.E. and Huntington, S.P. (eds) (2000), *Culture Matters: How Values Shape Human Progress* (New York: Basic Books).

Heide, J.B. and Milner, A.S. (1992), 'The Shadow of the Future: Effects of Anticipated Interaction and Frequency of Contacts in Buyer-Seller Cooperation', *Academy of Management Journal* 35:2, 265–91.

Heide, J.B. and Stump, R.L. (1995), 'Performance Implications of Buyer-Supplier Relationships in Industrial Markets: A Transaction Cost Explanation', *Journal of Business Research* 32, 57–66.

Heide, J.B. and Wathne, K.H. (2006), 'Friends, Businesspeople, and Relationship Roles: A Conceptual Framework and a Research Agenda', *Journal of Marketing* 70, 90–103.

Hendley, K. (1999), 'Rewriting the Rules of the Game in Russia: The Neglected Issue of the Demand for Law', *East European Constitutional Review* 8:4, 89–95.

Hendley, K. (2001), 'Beyond the Tip of the Iceberg: Business Disputes in Russia', in *Assessing the Value of Law in Transition Economies* (ed.) P. Murrell (Ann Arbor: University of Michigan Press), 20–55.

Hendley, K. (2004), 'The Rule of Law and Economic Development in the Global Era', in *The Blackwell Companion to Law and Society* (ed.) A. Sarat (Malden, USA: Blackwell), 605–23.

Hendley, K., Murrell, P. and Ryterman, R. (2000), 'Law, Relationships, and Private Enforcement: Transactional Strategies of Russian Enterprises', *Europe-Asia Studies* 52, 627–56.

Hendley, K., Murrell, P. and Ryterman, R. (2001), 'Law Works in Russia: The Role of Law in Interenterprise Transactions', in *Assessing the Value of Law in Transition Economies* (ed.) P. Murrell (Ann Arbor: University of Michigan Press), 56–93.

Hennart, J.-F. (1993), 'Explaining the Swollen Middle; Why Most Transactions are a Mix of Market and Hierarchy', *Organization Science* 4, 529–48.

Hilaire, J. (1964), 'Nos ancêtres les Gaulois', *Annales africaines* 7–77.

Hillman, R.A. (1997), *The Richness of Contract Law: An Analysis and Critique of Contemporary Theories of Contract Law* (Dordrecht: Kluwer Academic Publishing).

Hirowatari, S. (2000), 'Post-War Japan and the Law: Mapping Discourses of Legalization and Modernization', *Social Science Japan Journal* 3, 115–69.

Hofstede, G.H. (1980), *Culture's Consequences: International Differences in Work-Related Values* (Newbury Park, CA: Sage).

Huntington, S.P. (1996), *The Clash of Civilizations and the Remaking of World Order* (New York: Simon & Schuster).

Issa-Sayegh, J. (1997), 'L'intégration juridique des états africains de la zone franc', *Recueil Penant* 107: 823, 5–31.

Issa-Sayegh, J. (1999), 'L'OHADA instrument d'intégration juridique des pays africains de la zone franc', *Revue de jurisprudence commerciale* 6, 237–45.

Issa-Sayegh, J. (2001), 'L'OHADA: Bilan et perspectives', *International Law FORUM du droit international* 3, 156–62.

Issa-Sayegh, J. and Lohoues-Oble, J. (2002), *OHADA, Harmonisation du droit des affaires* (Bruxelles: Bruylant).

Jackson, T. (2004), *Management and Change in Africa: A Cross-Cultural Perspective* (London: Routledge).

Jeol, M. (1963), *La réforme de la justice en Afrique noire* (Paris: Éditions A. Pedone).

John-Nambo, J. (2002), 'Quelques héritages de la justice coloniale en Afrique noire', *Droit et Société* 51–2, 325–44.

Johnson, S., McMillan, J. and Woodruff, C. (2002), 'Courts and Relational Contracts', *Journal of Law, Economics & Organization* 18, 221–77.

Jones, C.A.G. (1994), 'Capitalism, Globalization and Rule of Law: An Alternative Trajectory of Legal Change in China', *Social and Legal Studies* 3, 195–221.

Kabou, A. (1991), *Et si l'Afrique refusait le développement?* (Paris: L'Harmattan).

Kahn-Freund, O. (1974), 'On Uses and Misuses of Comparative Law', *Modern Law Review* 37, 1–27.

Kali, R. (2001), 'Business Networks in Transition Economies: Norms, Contracts, and Legal Institutions', in *Assessing the Value of Law in Transition Economies* (ed.) P. Murrell (Ann Arbor: University of Michigan Press), 211–28.

Kamann, D.-J.F., Snidjers, C., Tazelaar, F. and Welling, D.T. (2006), 'The Ties that Bind: Buyer-Supplier Relations in the Construction Industry', *Journal of Purchasing and Supply Management* 12, 28–38.

Kamto, M. (1987), *Pouvoir et droit en Afrique noire* (Paris: Librairie générale de droit et de jurisprudence).

Kamto, M. (1990), 'Une justice entre tradition et modernité', *Afrique contemporaine* 156, 57–64.

Karlan, D. and Appel, J. (2011), *More than Good Intentions: How a New Economics is Helping to Solve Global Poverty* (New York: Dutton).

Kawashima, T. (1963), 'Dispute Resolution in Contemporary Japan', in *Law in Japan: The Legal Order of a Changing Society* (ed.) A.T.v. Mehren (Cambridge: Harvard University Press), 41–60.

Keefer, P. and Knack, S. (2005), 'Social Capital, Social Norms and the New Institutional Economics', in *Handbook of New Institutional Economics* (eds) C. Menard and M.M. Shirley (Dordrecht: Springer), 701–25.

Kenfack Douajni, G. (1998), 'Les conditions de la création, dans l'espace OHADA, d'un environnement juridique favorable au développement', *Revue juridique et politique, indépendance et coopération* 52, 39–47.

Kenworthy, L., Macaulay, S. and Rogers, J. (1996), '"The More Things Chang ...": Business Litigation and Governance in the American Automobile Industry', *Law and Social Inquiry* 21, 631–78.

Kirsch, M. (1998), 'Historique de l'Organisation pour l'harmonisation en Afrique du droit des affaires (OHADA)', *Recueil Penant* 108:827, 129–35.

Knack, S. and Keefer, P. (1997), 'Does Social Capital Have an Economic Payoff? A Cross-Country Investigation', *The Quarterly Journal of Economics* 112, 1251–88.

Konde, K., Kuyu, C. and Le Roy, É. (2002), 'Demandes de justice et accès au droit en Guinée', *Droit et Société* 51–2, 383–93.

Korobkin, R. (2002), 'Empirical Scholarship in Contract Law: Possibilities and Pitfalls', *University of Illinois Law Review* 1033–66.

Krippner, G.R. (2001), 'The Elusive Market: Embeddedness and the Paradigm of Economic Sociology', *Theory and Society* 30, 775–810.

Krippner, G.R. and Alvarez, A.S. (2007), 'Embeddedness and the Intellectual Projects of Economic Sociology', *Annual Review of Sociology* 33, 219–40.

Kritzer, H.M. (1991), 'Propensity to Sue in England and the United States: Blaming and Claiming in Tort Cases', *Journal of Law and Society* 18, 400–427.

La Porta, R., López-de-Silanes, F., Shleifer, A. and Vishny, R. (1998), 'Law and Finance', *Journal of Political Economy* 106, 1113–55.

La Porta, R., López-de-Silanes, F., Shleifer, A. and Vishny, R. (1999), 'The Quality of Government', *Journal of Law, Economics and Organization* 15, 222–79.

Labazée, P. (1995), 'Entreprises, promoteurs et rapports communautaires: les logiques économiques de la gestion des liens sociaux', in *Entreprises et entrepreneurs africains* (eds) S. Ellis and Y.-A. Fauré (Paris: Karthala), 141–53.

Landa, J.T. (1994), *Trust, Ethnicity, and Identity: Beyond the New Institutional Economics of Ethnic Trading Networks, Contract Law and Gift-Exchange* (Ann Arbor: University of Michigan Press).

Landa, J.T. (2001), 'Coasean Foundations of a Unified Theory of Western and Chinese Contractual Practices and Economic Organisations', in *Rules and Networks: The Legal Culture of Global Business Transactions* (eds) R.P. Appelbaum, W.L.F. Felstiner and V. Gessner (Oxford, Portland, Oregon: Hart), 347–62.

Landes, D. (2000), 'Culture Makes Almost All the Difference', in *Culture Matters: How Values Shape Human Progress* (eds) L.E. Harrison and S.P. Huntington (New York: Basic Books), 2–13.

Le Roy, É. (1999), *Le jeu des lois – Une anthropologie dynamique du Droit* (Paris: LGDJ).

Lecarme-Frassy, M. (2000), *Marchandes dakaroises entre maison et marché: approche anthropologique* (Paris: L'Harmattan).

Lecointre, G. (1993), 'Etudiants et cadres sénégalais: quelques aspects socioculturels de leurs mentalités et comportements', in *Esprit d'entreprise. Aspects managériaux dans le monde francophone* (eds) B. Ponson and J.-L. Schaan (Paris: John Libbey Eurotexte), 61–80.

Ledongo, P. (2010), 'Statistiques de la CCJA en matière contentieuse, arbitrale et consultative en dix ans de fonctionnement', *Revue de droit uniforme africain*, 62.

Lee, J.M. (1967), *Colonial Development and Good Government* (Oxford: Oxford University Press).

Leeson, P.T. (2006), 'Cooperation and Conflict: Evidence on Self-Enforcing Arrangements and Heterogeneous Groups', *American Journal of Economics and Sociology* 65, 891–907.

Legrand, P. (2001), 'What "Legal Transplants"?', in *Adapting Legal Cultures* (eds) D. Nelken and J. Feest (Oxford: Hart Publications), 55–70.

Leys, C. (1996), *The Rise and Fall of Development Theory* (London: James Currey).

Lugard, L. (1965), *The Dual Mandate in British Tropical Africa*, 5th edn (London: Frank Cass & Co).

M'Baye, K. (1966), 'Droit et développement en Afrique francophone de l'Ouest', in *Les aspects juridiques du développement économique – Legal Aspects of Economic Development* (ed.) A. Tunc (Paris: Dalloz), 121–65.

M'Baye, K. (2004), 'L'histoire et les objectifs de l'OHADA', *Petites affiches – la loi*, 205, 4–7.

Macaulay, S. (1963), 'Non-Contractual Relations in Business: A Preliminary Study', *American Sociological Review* 28, 1–19.

Macaulay, S. (1985), 'An Empirical View of Contract', *Wisconsin Law Review* 3, 465–82.

Macaulay, S. (1995), 'Crime and Custom in Business Society', *Journal of Law and Society* 22, 248–58.

Macaulay, S. (1996), 'Organic Transactions: Contract, Frank Lloyd Wright and the Johnson Building', *Wisconsin Law Review*, 74–121.

Macaulay, S. (2000), 'Relational Contracts Floating on a Sea of Custom? Thoughts About the Ideas of Ian Macneil and Lisa Bernstein', *Northwestern University Law Review* 94, 775–804.

Macaulay, S. (2003), 'The Real and the Paper Deal: Empirical Pictures of Relationships, Complexity and the Urge for Transparent Simple Rules', *Modern Law Review* 66, 44–79.

Macaulay, S. (2004), 'Freedom From Contract: Solutions in Search of a Problem?', *Wisconsin Law Review*, 777–820.

Macaulay, S. (2006), 'Contracts, New Legal Realism, and Improving the Navigation of *The Yellow Submarine*', *Tulane Law Review* 80, 1161–96.

Macneil, I.R. (1980), *The New Social Contract: An Inquiry into Modern Contractual Relations* (New Haven: Yale University Press).

Macneil, I.R. (1985), 'Relational Contract: What we do and do not Know', *Wisconsin Law Review* 3, 483–525.

Macneil, I.R. (2000), 'Relational Contract Theory: Challenges and Queries', *Northwestern University Law Review* 94, 877–907.

Maine, H.S. (1861), *Ancient Law: Its Connection to the History of Early Society* (London: John Murray).

Mair, L.P. (1936), *Native Policies in Africa* (London: George Routledge & Sons).

Malhotra, D. and Murnighan, J.K. (2002), 'The Effects of Contracts on Interpersonal Trust', *Administrative Science Quarterly* 47, 534–59.

Malinowski, B. (1951), *Crime and Custom in Savage Society* (New York: The Humanities Press).

Mamdani, M. (1996), *Citizen and Subject: Contemporary Africa and the Legacy of Late Colonialism* (Princeton: Princeton University Press).

Mann, K. and Roberts, R. (ed.) (1991), *Law in Colonial Africa* (London: James Currey), 3–58.

March, J.G. (1994), *A Primer on Decision-Making: How Decisions Happen* (New York: The Free Press).

Marfaing, L. and Sow, M. (1998), 'Les commerçants sénégalais et le commerce des années 1930 à nos jours: entre le formel et l'informel. Structures parallèles/ informelles: du dualisme à l'interdépendance', in *Les opérateurs économiques et l'État au Sénégal* (eds) L. Harding, L. Marfaing and M. Sow (Hamburg: LIT), 27–48.

Marfaing, L. and Sow, M. (1999), *Les opérateurs économiques au Sénégal. Entre le formel et l'informel 1930-1996.* (Paris: Karthala).

Marshall, H.H. (1966), 'The Changes and Adjustments Which Should be Made to the Present Legal Systems of the Newly Independent Countries of Africa to Permit Them to Respond More Effectively to the New Requirements of the Development of Such Countries', in *Les aspects juridiques du développement économique – Legal Aspects of Economic Development* (ed.) A. Tunc (Paris: Dalloz), 75–120.

Martor, B., Pilkington, N., Sellers, D.S. and Thouvenot, S. (2002), *Business Law in Africa: OHADA and the Harmonization Process* (London: Eversheds, Kogan Page).

Mattei, U. (1997), 'Three Patterns of Law: Taxonomy and Change in the World's Legal Systems', *American Journal of Comparative Law* 45, 5–44.

McAuslan, P. (1997), 'Law, Governance and the Development of the Market: Practical Problems and Possible Solutions', in *Good Government and the Law* (ed.) J. Faundez (New York: St.Martin's Press), 25–44.

McAuslan, P. (2002), 'Path Dependency, Law and Development', *Journal of Commonwealth Law and Legal Education* 1, 51–68.

McMillan, J. (2002), *Reinventing the Bazaar: A Natural History of Markets* (New York: W.W. Norton).

McMillan, J. and Woodruff, C. (1999), 'Dispute Prevention without Courts in Vietnam', *Journal of Law, Economics, and Organization* 15:3, 637–58.

McMillan, J. and Woodruff, C. (2000), 'Private Ordering Under Dysfunctional Public Order', *Michigan Law Review* 98, 2421–58.

Meagher, K. (2005), 'Social Capital or Analytical Liabilities? Social Networks and African Informal Economies', *Global Networks* 5, 217–38.

Meagher, K. (2006), 'Social Capital, Social Liabilities and Political Capital: Social Networks and Informal Manufacturing in Nigeria', *African Affairs* 105, 553–82.

Meagher, K. (2007), 'Manufacturing Disorder: Liberalization, Informal Enterprise and Economic "Ungovernance" in African Small Firm Clusters', *Development and Change* 38, 473–503.

Meillassoux, C. (ed.) (1971), *The Development of Indigenous Trade and Markets in Africa / L'évolution du commerce en Afrique de l'Ouest. Studies Presented and Discussed at the Tenth International African Seminar, Fourah Bay College, Freetown, December 1969* (Oxford: Oxford University Press for the International African Institute).

Merry, S.E. (1991), 'Law and Colonialism', *Law and Society Review* 25, 889–922.

Merry, S.E. (1992), 'Anthropology, Law, and Transnational Processes', *Annual Review of Anthropology* 21, 357–79.

Merry, S.E. (1999), 'Pluralizing Paradigms: From Gluckman to Foucault', *Political and Legal Anthropology Review* 22, 115–22.

Merry, S.E. (2003), 'From Law and Colonialism to Law and Globalization: A Review Essay on Martin Chanock, *Law, Custom, and Social Order: The Colonial Experience in Malawi and Zambia*', *Law and Social Inquiry* 28, 569–90.

Merry, S.E. (2004), 'Colonial and Postcolonial Law', in *The Blackwell Companion to Law and Society* (ed.) A. Sarat (Malden, MA: Blackwell Publishing), 569–88.

Merryman, J.H. (1977), 'Comparative law and Social Change: On the Origins, Style, Decline & Revival of the Law and Development Movement', *American Journal of Comparative Law* 27, 457–83.

Messick, R.E. (1997), 'Judicial Reform and Economic Development: A Survey of the Issues', *The World Bank Research Observer*, Feb 1997, 117–136.

Milgrom, P.R., North, D.C. and Weingast, B.R. (1990), 'The Role of Institutions in the Revival of Trade: The Law Merchant, Private Judges, and the Champagne Fairs', *Economics and Politics* 2, 1–23.

Mizruchi, M.S. and Brewster Stearns, L. (2001), 'Getting Deals Done: The Use of Social Networks in Bank Decision Making', *American Sociological Review* 66, 647–71.

Mohan, G. and Holland, J. (2001), 'Human Rights & Development in Africa: Moral Intrusion or Empowering Opportunities?' *Review of African Political Economy* 88, 177–96.

Mommsen, W.J. and De Moor, J.A. (ed.) (1992), *European Expansion and the Law* (Oxford: Berg).

Montesquieu, C.L. (1748), *De l'Esprit des Lois* (Genève: Barrillot & Fils).

Montgomery, J.D. (1998), 'Toward a Role-Theoretic Conception of Embeddedness', *American Journal of Sociology* 104–125, 92.

N'Dione, E.S. (1994), *L'économie urbaine en Afrique: le don et le recours* (Paris: Karthala).

N'Doye, D. (1995), 'OHADA, mythe et réalité', *Revue internationale de droit africain EDJA* 27, 7–8.

Nkou Mvondo, P. (2002), 'La Justice parallèle au Cameroun: la réponse des populations camerounaises à la crise de la Justice de l'État', *Droit et Société* 51–2, 369–81.

North, D.C. (1990), *Institutions, Institutional Change and Economic Performance* (Cambridge: Cambridge University Press).

North, D.C. (2005), 'Institutions and the Performance of Economies over Time', in *Handbook of New Institutional Economics* (eds) C. Menard and M.M. Shirley (Dordrecht: Springer), 21–30.

Nwabueze, B.O. (1966), 'Legal Aspects of Economic Development', in *Les aspects juridiques du développement économique – Legal Aspects of Economic Development* (ed.) A. Tunc (Paris: Dalloz), 167–91.

Ofosu-Amaah, W.P. (2000), *Reforming Business-Related Laws to Promote Private Sector Development: The World Bank Experience in Africa* (Washington, DC: World Bank).

OHADA (Directoire) (1994), *L'harmonisation du droit des affaires en Afrique. Outil technique de l'intégration économique.*

OHADA (1997), 'Treaty on the Harmonisation of Business Law in Africa', *Journal Officiel de l'OHADA*, no. 4, 1 November 1997.

Opoku, K. (1974), 'Traditional Law Under French Colonial Rule', *Verfassung und Recht in Übersee* 7, 139–53.

Paillusseau, J. (1999), 'Une révolution juridique en Afrique francophone', in *Mélanges M. Jeantin* (Paris: Dalloz), 93–100.

Paillusseau, J. (2004), 'Le droit de l'OHADA: un droit très important et original', *JCP - Cahiers de droit de l'entreprise*, 1–5.

Perry, A. (2000), 'Effective Legal Systems and Foreign Direct Investment: In Search of the Evidence', *The International and Comparative Law Quarterly* 49, 779–99.

Phillips, Arthur (1956), 'The Future of Customary Law in Africa' in *The Future of Customary Law in Africa – L'avenir du droit coutumier en Afrique* (Leiden: Universitaire Pers Leiden), 88–101.

Pistor, K. (1999), 'Supply and Demand for Law in Russia', *East European Constitutional Review* 8:4, 105–8.

Pistor, K. (2001), 'Law as a Determinant for Equity Market Development: The Experience of Transition Economies', in *Assessing the Value of Law in Transition Economies* (ed.) P. Murrell (Ann Arbor: University of Michigan Press), 249–87.

Pistor, K. and Berkowitz, D. (2003), 'Of Legal Transplants, Legal Irritants, and Economic Development', in *Corporate Governance and Capital Flows in a Global Economy* (eds) P.K. Cornelius and B. Kogut (Oxford: Oxford University Press), 347–70.

Plattner, S. (1990), 'Equilibrating Market Relationships', in *Markets and Marketing* (ed.) S. Plattner (Lanham, MD: University Press of the Americas), 133–52.

Pleskovic, B. and Stiglitz, J.E. (eds) (1999), *Annual World Bank Conference on Development Economics 1999* (Washington, DC: World Bank).

Podolny, J.M. and Page, K.L. (1998), 'Network Forms of Organization', *Annual Review of Sociology* 24, 57–76.

Polanyi, K. (1957), *The Great Transformation* (Boston: Beacon Press).

Polo, A. (2000), *L'OHADA: Histoire, objectifs, structure* (Bruylant: Bruxelles).

Poppo, L. and Zenger, T. (2002), 'Do Formal Contracts and Relational Governance Function as Substitutes or Complements?' *Strategic Management Journal* 23, 707–25.

Portes, A. and Landolt, P. (2000), 'Social Capital: Promise and Pitfalls of its Role in Development', *Journal of Latin American Studies* 32, 529–47.

Portes, A. and Sensenbrenner, J. (1993), 'Embeddedness and Immigration: Notes on the Social Determinants of Economic Action', *The American Journal of Sociology* 98, 1320–50.

Posner, R. (1998), 'Creating a Legal Framework for Economic Development', *The World Bank Research Observer*, Feb 1998, 1–13.

Powell, W.W. (1990), 'Neither Market nor Hierarchy: Network Forms of Organization', in *Research in Organizational Behavior* (eds) B.M. Staw and L.L. Cummings (Greenwich, CT: JAI Press), 295–336.

Putnam, R.D., Leonardi, R. and Nanetti, R.Y. (1993), *Making Democracy Work: Civic Traditions in Italy* (Princeton, NJ: Princeton University Press).

Ranger, T. (1984), 'The Invention of Tradition in Colonial Africa', in *The Invention of Tradition* (eds) E. Hobsbawn and T. Ranger (Cambridge: Cambridge University Press), 211–62.

République du Sénégal (1999), *Stratégie de développement du secteur privé* (Dakar).

République du Sénégal (2007), *Situation économique et sociale de la région de Dakar, Année 2006* (Dakar).

République du Sénégal (2008), *Banque de données économiques et financières 2006, version définitive* (Dakar).

République du Sénégal (2010), *Étude sur l'offre et la demande de financement des PME au Sénégal* (Dakar).

Réussir (2009), 'CCIAD: Amadou Lamine Niang, candidat sortant appelle à des élections calmes', *Réussir* 23 décembre 2009.

Richman, B.D. (2004), 'Firms, Courts, and Reputation Mechanisms: Towards a Positive Theory of Private Ordering', *Columbia Law Review* 104, 2328–67.

Richman, B.D. (2006), 'How Communities Create Economic Advantage: Jewish Diamond Merchants in New York', *Law and Social Inquiry* 31, 383–420.

Robert, A. (1955), *L'évolution des coutumes de l'Ouest africain et la législation française* (Paris: Éditions de l'encyclopédie d'outre-mer).

Roberts-Wray, S.K. (1960), 'The Adaptation of Imported Law in Africa', *Journal of African Law* 4, 66–78.

Rolland, L. and Lampué, P. (1931), *Précis de législation coloniale (colonies, Algérie, protectorats, pays sous mandat)* (Paris: Dalloz).

Rooks, G., Raub, W. and Tazelaar, F. (2006), 'Ex Post Problems in Buyer-Supplier Transactions: Effects of Transaction Characteristics, Social Embeddedness, and Contractual Governance', *Journal of Management and Governance* 10:3, 239–76.

Rose, C.V. (1998), 'The 'New' Law and Development Movement in the Post-Cold War Era: A Vietnam Case Study', *Law and Society Review* 32, 93–140.

Rostow, W.W. (1960), *The Stages of Economic Growth: A Non-Communist Manifesto* (Cambridge: Cambridge University Press).

Rousseau, D.M. (1995), *Psychological Contracts in Organizations* (Thousand Oaks: Sage).

Rousseau, D.M., Sitkin, S.B., Burt, R.S. and Camerer, C. (1998), 'Introduction to Special Topic Forum: Not so Different after All: A Cross-Discipline View of Trust', *Academy of Management Review* 23, 393–404.

Saada, E. (2005), 'Entre "assimilation" et "décivilisation": L'imitation et le projet colonial républicain', *Terrain* 44, 19–38.

Saada, E. (2009), 'Penser le fait colonial à travers le droit en 1900', *Mil neuf cent. Revue d'histoire intellectuelle*, 27, 103–16.

Sabatini, F. (2006), 'The Empirics of Social Capital and Economic Development: A Critical Perspective', *Fondazione Eni Enrico Mattei Note di Lavoro Series* no 15.

Sako, M. (1998), 'Does Trust Improve Business Performance?', in *Trust Within and Between Organizations* (eds) C. Lane and R. Bachmann (Oxford: Oxford University Press), 88–117.

Salacuse, J.W. (1969), *An Introduction to Law in French-Speaking Africa* (Charlottesville, VA: The Michie Company).

Salamone, F.A. (1998), 'The Waziri and the Thief – Hausa Islamic Law in a Yoruba City, a Case Study from Ibadan, Nigeria', *Journal of Legal Pluralism and Unofficial Law* 42, 139–56.

Sandelowski, M. (1995), 'Sample Size in Qualitative Research', *Research in Nursing and Health* 18, 179–83.

Sanders, J. and Hamilton, V.L. (1992), 'Legal Cultures and Punishment Repertoires in Japan, Russia, and the United States', *Law and Society Review* 26 (s), 117–38.

Sané, I. (2003), *Le commerce para-global des 'baol baol': une économie globale dans le cadre du mouridisme* (Dakar: Goethe Institut Inter Nationes).

Schaeffer, E. (1974), 'Aliénation-Réception-Authenticité: Réflexions sur le droit du développement', *Recueil Penant* 84, 311–32.

Schiller, A.A. (1966), 'The Changes and Adjustments Which Should be Brought to the Present Legal Systems of the Countries of Africa to Permit Them to Respond More Effectively to the new Requirements of the Development of the Countries', in *Les aspects juridiques du développement économique – Legal Aspects of Economic Development* (ed.) A. Tunc (Paris: Dalloz), 193–202.

Schiller, A.A. (1968), 'Introduction', in *Africa and Law: Developing Legal Systems in African Commonwealth Nations* (ed.) T.W. Hutchison (Madison: University of Wisconsin Press), vii–xviii.

Scott, R.E. (2000), 'The Case for Formalism in Relational Contract', *Northwestern University Law Review* 94, 847–76.

Scott, R.E. (2004), 'The Death of Contract Law', *University of Toronto Law Journal* 54, 369–90.

Seidman, A.W. and Seidman, R.B. (1978), *On the Theory of Law and Development* (Institute for Development Studies, University of Nairobi).

Seidman, R.B. (1966), 'Law and Economic Development in Independent, English-Speaking, Sub-Saharan Africa', *Wisconsin Law Review* 999–1070.

Seidman, R.B. (1978), *The State, Law, and Development* (New York: St.Martin's Press).

Seidman, R.B. (1981), 'Law, Development and Legislative Drafting in English-Speaking Africa', *The Journal of Modern African Studies* 19, 133–61.

Seidman, R.B., Seidman, A. and Walde, T.W. (eds) (1999), *Making Development Work: Legislative Reform for Institutional Transformation and Good Governance* (The Hague: Kluwer Law International).

Sen, A. (2000), *What is the Role of Legal and Judicial Reform in the Development Process?* Paper delivered at the World Bank Legal Conference, Washington, DC, 5 June 2000.

Sen, A. (2001), *Development as Freedom* (Oxford University Press).

Sen, A. (2004), 'How does Culture Matter?', in *Culture and Public Action* (eds) V. Rao and M. Walton (Stanford, CA: Stanford University Press), 37–58.

Serageldin, I. and Taboroff, J. (eds) (1992), *Culture and Development in Africa* (Washington, DC: World Bank).

Shirley, M.M. (2005), 'Institutions and Development', in *Handbook of New Institutional Economics* (eds) C. Menard and M.M. Shirley (Dordrecht: Springer), 611–38.

Snyder, F.G. (1981), 'Colonialism and Legal Form – The Creation of "Customary Law" in Senegal', *Journal of Legal Pluralism and Unofficial Law* 19, 49–90.

Solus, H. (1927), *Traité de la condition des indigènes en droit privé* (Paris: Sirey).

Stephenson, M.C. (2000), 'A Trojan Horse Behind Chinese Walls?: Problems and Prospects of US-Sponsored "Rule of Law" Reform Projects in the People's Republic of China', *UCLA Pacific Basin Law Journal* 18, 64–97.

Stiglitz, J. (1997), 'The Role of Government in the Economies of Developing Countries', in *Development Strategy and the Management of the Market Economy* (ed.) E. Malinvaud (Clarendon Press for the United Nations), 61–109.

Stiglitz, J.E. (1999), 'Formal and Informal Institutions', in *Social Capital: A Multifaceted Perspective* (eds) P. Dasgupta and I. Serageldin (Washington, DC: World Bank), 59–70.

Stoufflet, J. (1962), 'De l'élaboration d'une législation de droit privé dans un pays en voie de développement', *Annales africaines* 250–55.

Tamanaha, B. (1995), 'The Lessons of Law-and-Development Studies', *American Journal of International Law* 89, 470–86.

Tamanaha, B.Z. (1999), 'A Pragmatic Approach to Legislative Theory for Developing Countries', in *Making Development Work: Legislative Reform for Institutional Transformation and Good Governance* (eds) R.B. Seidman, A. Seidman and T.W. Walde (The Hague/Boston: Kluwer Law International), 145–56.

Teubner, G. (1998), 'Legal Irritants: Good Faith in British Law or How Unifying Law Ends up in New Divergences', *Modern Law Review* 61, 11–32.

The Economist (2000), 'Hopeless Africa' (cover story), 13 May 2000, 17.

The Economist (2011), 'Africa Rising' (cover story), 3 December 2011, 15.

Thioub, I. (1998), 'A propos de la plate-forme revendicatrice de l'Union nationale des Commerçants et Industriels du Sénégal', in *Les opérateurs économiques et l'État au Sénégal* (eds) L. Harding, L. Marfaing and M. Sow (Hamburg: LIT), 127–47.

Thioub, I., Diop, M.-C. and Boone, C. (1998), 'Economic Liberalization in Senegal: Shifting Politics of Indigenous Business Interests', *African Studies Review* 41, 63–89.

Tiger, P. (2001), *Le droit des affaires en Afrique (OHADA)* (Paris: PUF).

Transparency International (2011), *Corruption Perceptions Index 2011* (Berlin: Transparency International).

Trebilcock, M. and Leng, J. (2006), 'The Role of Formal Contract Law and Enforcement in Economic Development', *Virginia Law Review* 92, 1517–80.

Trebilcock, M.J. (1997), 'What Makes Poor Countries Poor? : The Role of Institutional Capital in Economic Development', in *The Law and Economics of Development* (eds) E. Buscaglia, W. Ratliff and R. Cooter (Greenwich: JAI Press), 15–58.

Trubek, D.M. (1982), 'Toward a Social Theory of Law: An Essay on the Study of Law and Development', *Yale Law Journal*, 82, 1–50.

Trubek, D.M. (2001), 'Law and Development', in *International Encyclopedia of the Social and Behavioral Sciences* (eds) N.J. Smelser and P.B. Baltes (Oxford: Pergamon), 8443–6.

Trubek, D.M. (2006), 'The "Rule of Law" in Development Assistance: Past, Present, and Future', in *The New Law and Economic Development: A Critical Appraisal* (eds) D.M. Trubek and A. Santos (New York: Cambridge University Press), 74–94.

Trubek, D.M. and Galanter, M. (1974), 'Scholars in Self-Estrangement: Some Reflections on the Crisis in Law and Development Studies in the United States', *Wisconsin Law Review* 1062–102.

Trubek, D.M. and Santos, A. (2006), 'Introduction: The Third Moment in Law and Development Theory and the Emergence of a New Critical Practice', in *The*

New Law and Economic Development: A Critical Appraisal (eds) D.M. Trubek and A. Santos (New York: Cambridge University Press), 1–18.

Trubek, D.M. and Santos, A. (eds) (2006), *The New Law and Economic Development: A Critical Appraisal* (New York: Cambridge University Press).

Trubisky, P., Ting-Tommey, S. and Lin, S.-L. (1991), 'The Influence of Individualism, Collectivism and Self-Monitoring on Conflict Styles', *International Journal of Intercultural Relations* 15, 65–84.

Tunc, A. (1966), 'Les aspects juridiques du développement économique', in *Les aspects juridiques du développement économique – Legal Aspects of Economic Development* (ed.) A. Tunc (Paris: Dalloz), 1–24.

UEMOA (2004), *Le secteur informel dans les principales agglomérations de sept États membres de l'UEMOA: Performances, insertions, perspectives* (Bamako: Afristat).

UNIDA (2007a), 'Rapport Doing Business / Banque mondiale', *Lettre d'information OHADA.com du 15 février 2007*. Available at: http://www.ohada.com/actualite/123/rapport-doing-business-banque-mondiale.html.

UNIDA (2007b), 'Rapport Doing Business / Réponse de la Banque mondiale à la newsletter du 15 février 2007', *Lettre d'information OHADA.com du 27 février 2007*. Available at: http://www.ohada.com/actualite/129/rapport-doing-business-reponse-de-la-banque-mondiale-a-la-newsletter-du-15-fevrier-2007.html.

UNIDO (2002), *Foreign Direct Investor Perceptions in Sub-Saharan Africa* (Vienna: UNIDO).

UNIDO (2006), *Africa Foreign Investor Survey 2005: Understanding the Contributions of Different Investor Categories to Development – Implications for Targeting Strategies* (Vienna: UNIDO).

Upham, F. (1994), 'Speculations on Legal Informality: On Winn's "Relational Practices and the Marginalization of Law"', *Law and Society Review* 28, 233–41.

Upham, F. (2006), 'Mythmaking in the Rule-of-Law Orthodoxy', in *Promoting the Rule of Law Abroad: In Search of Knowledge* (ed.) T. Carothers (Washington, DC: Carnegie Endowment For International Peace), 75–104.

Uzzi, B. (1996), 'The Sources and Consequences of Embeddedness for the Economic Performance of Organizations: The Network Effect', *American Sociological Review* 61, 674–98.

Uzzi, B. (1997), 'Social Structure and Competition in Interfirm Networks: The Paradox of Embeddedness', *Administrative Sciences Quarterly* 42, 35–67.

Uzzi, B. (1999), 'Embeddedness in the Making of Financial Capital: How Social Relations and Networks Benefit Firms Seeking Financing', *American Sociological Review* 64, 481–505.

Uzzi, B. and Gillespie, J.J. (1999), 'Corporate Social Capital and the Cost of Financial Capital: An Embeddedness Approach', in *Corporate Social Capital and Liability* (eds) R.T.A.J. Leenders and S.M. Gabbay (Boston: Kluwer), 446–59.

Uzzi, B. and Lancaster, R. (2003), 'Relational Embeddedness and Learning: The Case of Bank Loan Managers and Their Clients', *Management Science*, 49, 383–99.

Vanderlinden, J. (2000), 'Les droits africains entre positivisme et pluralisme', *Bulletin des séances de l'Académie royale des sciences d'outre-mer* 46, 279–92.

Vincent-Jones, P. (1989), 'Contracts and Business Transactions: A Socio-Legal Analysis', *Journal of Law and Society* 16, 166–86.

Watson, A. (1993), *Legal Transplants: An Approach to Comparative Law*, 2nd edn (Athens, GA: University of Georgia Press).

Weintraub, R.J. (1992), 'A Survey of Contract Practice and Policy', *Wisconsin Law Review*, 1–60.

West, M.D. (2000), 'Private Ordering at the World's First Futures Exchange', *Michigan Law Review* 98, 2574–615.

Williamson, O.E. (1975), *Markets and Hierarchies: Analysis and Antitrust Implications* (New York: Free Press).

Williamson, O.E. (1985), *The Economic Institutions of Capitalism: Firms, Markets, Relational Contracting* (New York: Free Press).

Williamson, O.E. (1993), 'Calculativeness, Trust and Economic Organization', *Journal of Law and Economics* 36, 453–86.

Williamson, O.E. (1994), 'Transaction Cost Economics and Organization Theory', in *The Handbook of Economic Sociology* (eds) N.J. Smelser and R. Swedberg (Princeton, N.J.: Princeton University Press), 77–107.

Winn, J.K. (1994), 'Relational Practices and the Marginalization of Law: Informal Financial Practices of Small Businesses in Taiwan', *Law and Society Review* 28, 193–232.

Woodman, G.R. and Obilade, A.O. (eds) (1995), *African Law and Legal Theory* (New York: New York University Press).

Woodruff, C. (1998), 'Contract Enforcement and Trade Liberalization in Mexico's Footwear Industry', *World Development* 26, 979–91.

Woolcock, M. (1998), 'Social Capital and Economic Development: Toward a Theoretical Synthesis', *Theory and Society* 27, 151–208.

Woolthuis, R.K., Hillebrand, B. and Nooteboom, B. (2005), 'Trust, Contract and Relationship Development', *Organization Studies* 26, 813–40.

World Bank (1989), *Sub-Saharan Africa: From Crisis to Sustainable Growth* (Washington, DC: World Bank).

World Bank (1992), *Governance and Development* (Washington, DC: World Bank).

World Bank (1997), *World Development Report 1997: The State in a Changing World* (New York: Oxford University Press for the World Bank).

World Bank (2002), *World Development Report 2002: Building Institutions for Markets* (New York: Oxford University Press).

World Bank (2003), *Doing Business in 2004: Understanding Regulation* (Washington, DC: World Bank /Oxford University Press).

World Bank (2004a), *Enquête Climat des Investissements Auprès des Entreprises Informelles* [unpublished].

World Bank (2004b), *World Development Report 2005: A Better Investment Climate for Everyone* (New York: World Bank and Oxford University Press).

World Bank (2005a), *Sénégal: une évaluation du climat des investissements* (World Bank).

World Bank (2005b), 'Wolfowitz Points to Urgent Development Agenda' [Online]. Available at: http://go.worldbank.org/DXREB2FDT0.

World Bank (2008), *Doing Business 2009: Comparing Regulation in 181 Economies* (Palgrave Macmillan/World Bank).

World Bank (2012a), *Doing Business in 2012: Doing business in a more transparent world* (Washington, DC: World Bank).

World Bank (2012b), 'Social Capital' [Online]. Available at: http://go.worldbank.org/C0QTRW4QF0 [accessed: 5 April 2012].

World Bank Legal Vice Presidency (2004), *Initiatives in Legal and Judicial Reform* (Washington DC: World Bank).

Wuyts, S. and Geyskens, I. (2005), 'The Formation of Buyer-Supplier Relationships: Detailed Contract Drafting and Close Partner Selection', *Journal of Marketing* 69:4, 103–17.

Yngvesson, B. (1985), 'Re-Examining Continuing Relations and the Law', *Wisconsin Law Review* 623–46.

Zelizer, V.A. (2005), *The Purchase of Intimacy* (Princeton, N.J.: Princeton University Press).

Index